NATIONAL U

D0722174

053176

DIVORCE AND FAMILY MEDIATION

James C. Hansen, Editor
Sarah Childs Grebe, Volume Editor

The Family Therapy Collections

AN ASPEN PUBLICATION®
Aspen Systems Corporation
Rockville, Maryland
Royal Tunbridge Wells
1985

Library of Congress Cataloging in Publication Data
Main entry under title:

Divorce and family mediation.

(The Family therapy collections, ISSN 0735-9152; 12)
Includes bibliographies and index.
1. Divorce mediation—United States—Addresses, essays, lectures.
I. Hansen, James C. II. Series.
HQ834.D54   1985   306.8'9   84-21516
ISBN: 0-89443-611-2

Publisher: John R. Marozsan
Associate Publisher: Jack W. Knowles, Jr.
Editorial Director: Margaret Quinlin
Executive Managing Editor: Margot G. Raphael
Managing Editor: M. Eileen Higgins
Editorial Services: Ruth McKendry
Printing and Manufacturing: Debbie Collins

The Family Therapy Collections series is indexed in *Psychological Abstracts*
and the PsycINFO database

Copyright © 1985 by Aspen Systems Corporation
All rights reserved.

Aspen Systems Corporation grants permission for copies of articles in this
issue to be made for personal or internal use, or for the personal or internal
use of specific clients registered with the Copyright Clearance
Center (CCC). This consent is given on the condition, however, that the
copier pay a $2.50 fee for copying beyond that permitted by the
U.S. Copyright Law. The $2.50 fee should be paid directly to
the CCC, 21 Congress St., Salem, MA 01970.
0-89443-611-2/84 $2.50.

This consent does not extend to other kinds of copying, such as
copying for general distribution, for advertising or promotional
purposes, for creating new collective works, or for resale. For
information, address Aspen Systems Corporation, 1600 Research
Boulevard, Rockville, Maryland 20850.

Library of Congress Catalog Card Number: 84-21516
ISBN: 0-89443-611-2
ISSN: 0735-9152

Printed in the United States of America

1   2   3   4   5

Table of Contents

Board of Editors

Editor

JAMES C. HANSEN
State University of New York at Buffalo
Buffalo, New York

JAMES F. ALEXANDER
University of Utah
Salt Lake City, Utah

FLORENCE W. KASLOW
Kaslow Associates, P.A.
West Palm Beach, Florida

CAROLYN L. ATTNEAVE
University of Washington
Seattle, Washington

DAVID P. KNISKERN
University of Cincinnati
College of Medicine
Central Psychiatric Clinic
Cincinnati, Ohio

JOHN ELDERKIN BELL
Stanford University
Palo Alto, California

LUCIANO L'ABATE
Georgia State Univeristy
Atlanta, Georgia

HOLLIS A. EDWARDS
Toronto East General Hospital
Toronto Family Therapy Institute
Toronto, Ontario, Canada

KITTY LAPERRIERE
Ackerman Institute for Family
Therapy
Columbia University School of
Medicine
New York, New York

NATHAN B. EPSTEIN
Brown University
Butler Hospital
Providence, Rhode Island

ALAN S. GURMAN
University of Wisconsin
Medical School
Madison, Wisconsin

ARTHUR MANDELBAUM
The Menninger Foundation
Topeka, Kansas

AUGUSTUS Y. NAPIER
The Family Workshop
Atlanta, Georgia

JOHN HOWELLS
Institute of Family Psychiatry
Ipswich, England

Board of Editors
(continued)

Contributors

SARAH CHILDS GREBE
Family Center for Mediation and Counseling
Kinsington, Maryland

EDWARD BEAL, M.D.
Bethesda, Maryland

EMILY M. BROWN
Divorce and Marital Stress Clinic
Arlington, Virginia

SUSAN BROWN
Washington, D.C.

CATHERINE GRAYSON CROCKETT
Bethesda, Maryland

LORI HEYMAN GORDON
Center for Separation and Divorce
Mediation
Falls Church, Virginia

KAREN K. IRVIN
Minnesota Mediation and
Counseling Center
Minneapolis, Minnesota

ELIZABETH JANSSEN KOOPMAN
Institute for Child Study
The University of Maryland
College Park, Maryland

MARTIN KRANITZ
Annapolis, Maryland

ANN L. MILNE
Madison, Wisconsin

Preface

The Family Therapy Collections is a quarterly publication in which topics of current and specific interest to family therapists are presented. Each volume contains articles authored by practicing professionals, providing in-depth coverage of a single significant aspect of family therapy. This volume focuses on divorce mediation.

There is an increasing interest in the use of mediation for family conflicts, particularly with divorcing couples. Mediation is not therapy, nor is it the practice of law; however, it may be used as an alternative to the legal adversary approach. In divorce mediation, a neutral third person or persons help the divorcing couple to negotiate their own settlement. Mediation encourages cooperation and is intended to reduce the anger and bitterness that often arise in adversarial situations. Although this volume focuses on divorce mediation, the concepts and techniques are applicable in other family conflict situations.

In most cases, divorcing couples volunteer to participate in mediation. The mediator works with a couple with the understanding that it is their intention to break up the marriage. The mediator does not function as a lawyer, but is knowledgeable of the legal and tax implications of the couple's proposed settlement and usually encourages both parties to consult with attorneys. Frequently, mediators are either lawyers or family therapists; they may work as co-mediators. This volume differentiates mediation from therapy, and presents the concepts, processes, and techniques of mediation.

The editor of this volume is Sarah Childs Grebe. She is the Director of the Family Center for Mediation and Counseling in Kensington, Maryland. She is also an instructor at Catholic University in Washington, D.C., in the

Mediation Certificate Program and a trainer for the National Center for Mediation Education in Annapolis, Maryland. Ms. Grebe has selected skilled therapists and mediators to contribute articles that will be useful for therapists working with families in need of mediation. This volume may also stimulate therapists to seek additional specific training in mediation.

James C. Hansen
Editor

Introduction

Mediation, defined in Webster's dictionary as the "intercession or friendly intervention for settling differences between persons, nations, etc.," has existed as a distinct means of resolving disputes for thousands of years. Only recently, however, has mediation been suggested for resolving one unique type of dispute, that of marital dissolution.

The movement toward an alternative approach to divorce began with two major developments, one national and one local. In the 1960s, the divorce reform movement was born through the efforts of people all over the United States who worked to change their state statutes on divorce. Their primary goal was the passage of no fault divorce laws, which eliminate the need to place blame and punish one's spouse in order to terminate a marriage contract. In the early 1970s, an original experiment called The Bridge was conducted in Atlanta, Georgia. The Bridge provided parents and their runaway adolescents a neutral ground on which to resolve their differences with the aid of an impartial facilitator; the process they used was mediation. On the board of The Bridge was an attorney and family therapist named O.J. Coogler, who was impressed by the success of mediation at The Bridge. Searching for a way to help people avoid traumatic divorce, Coogler developed a Structured Mediation approach, a cooperative problem-solving approach to separation and divorce that has gained growing acceptance by the public and professionals alike.

The aim of this volume on mediation is to present the different aspects of mediation as they affect the family therapist dealing with divorce. In the lead article, Anne Milne, a mediator in Madison, Wisconsin, and the author of several articles on mediation, explores the differences and similarities in therapy and mediation. She defines and compares the goals and processes inherent in both disciplines, suggesting how each leads to the use of certain techniques with clients.

The second selection is by Edward Beal, a family therapist and clinical assistant professor at Georgetown University Medical School in Washington, D.C. He develops a systems view of three different strategies: therapy, mediation, and litigation for intervention in divorce.

In the third article, Sarah Childs Grebe reviews the various theories and schemata on the divorce process and analyzes their impact on the mediation process.

Susan Brown, formerly director of the National Center for Family Studies at Catholic University, Washington, D.C., has firsthand experience as a mediation client. She also has an interest in the ways that different models of mediation affect the outcome for individual clients.

Lori Heyman Gordon, director of The Family Relations Institute in Falls Church, Virginia, has developed an option for couples seeking mediation for separation and divorce that she calls marital assessment. Whether the couple reconciles or proceeds with the divorce, the assessment helps them understand more fully the reasons for their decision.

Co-mediation as an option is explored by Martin Kranitz, vocational counselor and mediator in Annapolis, Maryland, and mediation trainer for the National Center for Mediation Education. He discusses the different combinations of professions and sexes for co-mediation, as well as the ramifications of each.

Emily Brown, director of the Divorce and Marital Stress Clinic in Rosslyn, Virginia, describes emotional dynamics of couples who are utilizing mediation. She details ways of detecting behavior patterns and suggests ways to deal with them.

Karen Irvin is a mediator, therapist, and trainer in Minneapolis, Minnesota, where she specializes in working with children. She decribes the pitfalls and benefits of including children in divorce mediation and offers suggestions on ways to include them based on her own experience.

Catherine Crockett is a domestic relations lawyer and mediator in Bethesda, Maryland, and trainer in mediation for the National Center for Mediation Education. She addresses many of the legal questions that mediators and therapists working with divorcing couples must consider.

Elizabeth Koopman of the University of Maryland's Institute for Child Study writes on the many issues surrounding the appropriate education and training of mediators who work with divorcing couples and their families.

This collection brings together many of the persons directly involved in shaping and defining the field of mediation as it applies to separation and divorce. They are in mediation practice and, thus, have firsthand experience in the areas about which they chose to write. The field of mediation is growing and expanding daily, moving in many exciting directions. This collection is part of that growth.

Sarah Childs Grebe
Volume Editor

1. Mediation or Therapy— Which Is It?

Ann L. Milne

FAMILY CONFLICT HAS BEEN ADDRESSED BY A VARIETY OF PROFES-sionals using a diversity of interventions and techniques from a great many disciplines. The use of mediation as a technique for resolving conflict within the family, notably that between divorcing spouses, draws on the bodies of theory developed in anthropology, sociology, psychotherapy, theology, education, law, and philosophy. As mediation evolves into a distinct field of practice, it attracts practitioners from each of these disciplines. Confusion about definitions arises as techniques are borrowed from previously established models of conflict resolution and incorporated into the practice of mediation. A blurring is most noticeable among the practices of marital and family therapy, divorce counseling, and divorce mediation.

The study of the development of a field of practice provides an understanding of its definition and theory. Definition and theory, in turn, provide the foundation for process and dictate the practice and interventions that apply. Although psychotherapy and mediation both focus on the resolution of conflict, the conflict is defined and addressed in dissimilar ways.

HISTORY OF PSYCHOTHERAPY

Early psychotherapy included the treatment of fools, psychotics, and the feebleminded through the use of magic potions, medicines, banishment, and institutionalization. These primitive healing techniques for dysfunctional individuals were closely linked with religion and the confession of wrongdoing or with superstition and the use of magical incantations and concoctions (Silvano, 1974).

The confinement and institutionalization of disturbed individuals allowed a clinical observation of behavior and of the effect of various treatments. The resulting collection of experiences and rudimentary research produced a body of knowledge that was based not on religion and superstition but on more rational judgments of physical symptomatology. It was concluded that aberrations in behavior were the result of disturbances in blood, bile, and phlegm. Treatment included bloodletting and the administration of medicines. Primitive psychiatry evolved as a means of cataloging symptoms, causes, and treatment.

When it appeared that dysfunction was the result of disturbances in thought and passion, the physiological assessment and treatment of illness was expanded to include meditation, exercises in self-control, and the recitation of maxims. Therapy through thought control and words included support and consultation, with the elicitation of unconscious thoughts. Psychiatry as a biological science was later joined by psychoanalysis as a science that focused on the examination of thoughts and experiences (Enelow, 1977). The inclusion of experience as a determinant of behavior precipitated an explosion of new theory and methodology. A behavioral focus was added to the treatment of personality disturbance through insight and support.

Consideration of the patient system grew to include family, environment, and the patient's ability to function within a social system. Treatment of intrapersonal conflict was extended to treatment of interpersonal conflict. Individual therapy progressed to couples and family therapy, and the treatment of personality disorders grew to include the treatment of dysfunctional relationships. As the extended familial system evolved into a nuclear model, marriage and family counseling developed. Separation and divorce have now become remedies for interpersonal conflict and have led to the establishment of divorce counseling.

Psychotherapy has now evolved to include a plethora of models of treatment and interventions:

- insight therapies directed toward self-understanding and self-motivation
- supportive therapies directed toward self-actualization
- behavioral therapies directed toward the extinction of dysfunctional behavior and the reinforcement of functional behavior and interactions
- marital and family therapies directed toward the stabilization of intimate relationships

In spite of the diversity of the therapeutic schools of thought, the underlying principle is that of change. Therapists seek to change an individual or a relationship through the resolution of a crisis or trauma, through the acquisition of insight, through symptom relief, or through social rehabilitation. Although this goal may be reached by various means, depending on the method of treatment, therapy is considered successful when well-being and change are accomplished.

HISTORY OF DIVORCE MEDIATION

Interpersonal conflicts include disputes between individuals, neighbors, tribes, communities, and countries. Methods that have been used to resolve disputes include domination through physical force, duels, war, coin tosses, treaty negotiation, adjudication, and mediation. Although many definitions of mediation have been proposed, mediation as used in this paper is a means of resolving conflict through a neutral third party who facilitates communications, helps the parties in conflict define the issues, and works toward the resolution of those issues by assisting the disputants in their own negotiations (Milne, 1982; Milne, in press).

Mediation has been practiced in a variety of cultures. Gulliver (1979) traced the existence of mediation from primitive societies to the present. In Africa, an institution known as the community "moot" provided a type of mediation service to resolve a variety of interpersonal disputes. Mediation was a common means of resolving disputes in ancient China and is still used today to resolve certain issues, such as divorce and child custody disputes. Chinese immigrants to the United States in the mid-19th century brought this tradition with them, establishing the Chinese Benevolent Association to mediate disputes in their communities (Brown, 1982). The ancient Hebrews used a Jewish religious court that still exists today as the Jewish Conciliation Board, first established in 1920 in New York City, to help resolve disputes (Milne, 1982).

In 1974, Coogler, an attorney as well as a marriage and family counselor, established the Family Mediation Center in Atlanta, Georgia. Coogler (1978) began to institutionalize the idea of divorce mediation; he proposed a framework in which third party mediators used communication and intervention techniques borrowed from labor mediation and the social sciences to assist a divorcing couple in resolving contractual issues, such as finances, property division, support, and child custody. The focus of the interaction between the mediator and the couple changed from an examination of past events and causative factors to an examination of future needs and the development of a contractual agreement.

Coogler later established the Family Mediation Association as an organization of individuals interested in the development of divorce mediation as a viable means of resolving divorce-related disputes. Other organizations, such as the Academy of Family Mediators, have emerged to promote the concept of divorce mediation and to provide a network for practitioners. Each new publication and journal article adds to the definition and development of this new field of practice.

Modern forms of therapy emphasize the resolution of behavioral issues (e.g., working outside the home, financial arrangements, and parenting relationships) and future contractual relationships (e.g., conciliation agreements, prenuptial and postnuptial agreements, and mediated divorce stipulations). These behavioral and contractual forms of therapy address quasi-legal issues that reflect the growing awareness among individual and family therapists that relationships are not only psychogenic in nature but also psycholegal (Folberg & Milne, in press; Kaslow, 1979–1980; Kressel, Lopez-Morrilas, Weinglass, & Deutsch, 1978).

Most states now provide for some form of no fault divorce. The underlying premise of no fault divorce is that the parties involved rather than the court should be responsible for determining whether a divorce is warranted. This trend toward allowing the parties to retain their decision-making responsibilities is also found in the provisions for pro se divorce and joint custody. Each is premised on some degree of mutuality and cooperation, and each lessens the decision-making authority of the court (Milne, 1982; Milne, in press). The introduction of divorce mediation as a means for divorcing individuals to reach their own financial, property, and parental agreements continues the philosophy of returning decision making to the family (Milne, 1983).

The extension of mediation into the area of divorce is a natural progression consistent with the historical roots of mediation and the attitudinal and conceptual changes that have occurred in the social sciences and the law. Divorce mediation is unique because of the interdisciplinary nature of its development and the multidimensional nature of divorce. This multimodal aspect has caused confusion in actually defining divorce mediation.

Divorce mediation emerged as a specialty practice in the late 1970s and has continued to grow during the 1980s. There are a great many models of practice, styles, and techniques, which often reflect the previous profession and training of the mediator (Milne, 1981). As divorce mediation begins to move into its second developmental stage, we will undoubtedly see the promulgation of standards of practice. Research efforts will further define mediation, institutionalize a conceptual format, and provide methods and interventions that can be embraced by divorce mediators.

DIVORCE THERAPY VS. DIVORCE MEDIATION

The overall objective of psychotherapy is to establish internal harmony and effective intrapersonal and interpersonal functioning. It is generally accepted that personality disorders result primarily from interpersonal experiences, typically in early childhood, and are perpetuated through later growth and development.

A persistent theme of psychotherapy literature is that the development of insight through self-knowledge leads to emotional well-being (Singer, 1970). The psychotherapist attempts to establish a relationship with the patient, typically a parent-child relationship. As therapy progresses, the patient gains an understanding of the underlying issues and alters his or her personality structure. Classic psychoanalysis, as developed by Freud, is a long-term process and focuses on the individual; interpersonal relationships are of secondary importance (Olson, 1975; Singer, 1970). The briefer forms of insight therapies are more focused and time limited, often involving interpretation rather than insight to uncover past troubles and their effects on present day functioning (Enelow, 1977).

Unlike the insight therapies, behavioral therapy focuses on the patient's interactions within the current environment. Based on the principles of learning theory, this mode of therapy is intended to change behavior so that the patient develops a sense of well-being and functions at a more satisfactory level. The task is to change dysfunctional behavior patterns into desirable ones that will be maintained. Once the therapist has established a rapport with the client, a behavioral profile and a treatment plan are developed.

When therapy is extended to treatment of a couple or family, the goal continues to be the emotional well-being of the participants. This is accomplished through an enhanced understanding of the nature of the relationship, the origins of dissatisfaction, and the alteration of the family system. Improved communications, autonomy, individuation, and empathy are goals typically espoused by family therapists (Olson, 1975).

Divorce therapy has been described as a new profession or a new specialty within the existing profession of marriage and family therapy (Brown, 1976; Framo, 1978; Hunt, 1977). According to Brown (1982), divorce therapy

> is concerned with helping an individual or a couple disengage from the marital relationship, to adjust to the stress of separation, and to cope with such emotions as anger, hostility, resentment, anxiety, guilt, rejection, regret, grief, and depression. . . . Divorce therapy can also help individuals better understand what went wrong in their marriage, to help bridge the transition to single life, to prepare for future, post divorce relationships, including single parenting, and to be more aware of the effect of divorce on their children and the need of children for continuing relationships with both parents. (p. 30)

As the literature on divorce mediation grows, the distinction between divorce therapy and divorce mediation becomes clearer:

Divorce therapy may be differentiated from divorce mediation in that the former is focused more on stress relief, individual behavior change and increased self understanding, while the latter is focused more on dealing with specific problems, resolving disputes and negotiating differences inherent in the dissolution of the marital state. While successful divorce therapy may facilitate mediation and while successful mediation may be therapeutic, these two processes should be clearly separated. (Brown, 1982, pp. 30–31)

Conflict during a divorce, during a separation, or after a divorce brings the parties to divorce mediation. The focus of divorce mediation is on the dissolution of the marital corporation, including the allocation of the marital resources (e.g., property and finances) and the custody of children. The mediator guides the parties as they define the issues in dispute and negotiate an agreement. The parties retain control of the outcome rather than turn the decision making over to a judge or arbitrator (Milne, 1982).

Mediation is not treatment. The parties do not analyze past behaviors, but instead reach agreements that provide for the future (Milne, 1982). During mediation, there is no attempt to obtain insight into the history of conflict or to change personality patterns. Although these may both occur, they are fringe benefits of the mediation process (Folberg, 1983). The objective of mediation is to reach an agreement. Therapeutic interventions may be a means to that end, but they do not constitute the focus of the process as they do in therapy.

THE PROCESS OF MEDIATION

Several authors have described the mediation process as a linear series of stages (Brown, 1982; Gulliver, 1979; Moore, 1983). Kessler (1978) described mediation as a four-stage process: (1) setting the stage, (2) defining the issues, (3) processing the issues, and (4) resolving the issues.

Setting the Stage

The theater for mediation may have been established long before the disputants enter the mediator's office. Frustrations with the legal system, recommendations by friends and other professionals, and media attention may have alerted the couple to accept mediation as a means of resolving divorce-related conflicts. At the initial meeting between the couple and the mediator, the stage continues to be set as both the couple and the mediator gather data about each other, explore individual expectations, and formulate the beginning of the mediation relationship. This initial testing of the waters goes both ways—the clients assessing the mediator and the mediator assessing the clients.

Important here is the establishment of the relationship between the parties and the mediator based on a sense of trust, respect, empathy, and interest. As this is accomplished, the mediator builds credibility with the parties by explaining the mediation process, what it can and cannot accomplish, and how it may or may not be of help to them, based on their description of the issues in dispute.

By defining the mediator's role as that of a consultant who has contracted to facilitate the parties' communication and settlement process, the mediator indicates that he or she will assist them in reaching a resolution rather than determine a resolution for them. Experienced mediators emphasize that the final responsibility for settlement lies with the parties and that the job of the mediator is similar to that of a coach—calling a particular set of plays and strategies to assist the players on the field. As the clients become aware of their responsibility for the final outcome of mediation, they must confront their willingness to take risks and to trust each other. How vulnerable is each willing to be with the other? This question is answered by most couples according to the degree of trust they are willing to invest in the mediator and their sense of the mediator's expertise and understanding of them.

The mediator further sets the stage by foreshadowing (Kessler, 1978) some of the requirements of mediation (e.g., flexibility, a willingness to negotiate and compromise) and some of the typical stumbling blocks of mediation. This foreshadowing process helps the mediator define the task and helps the clients to commit themselves to the process (Kessler, 1978). As the parties assess the appropriateness of mediation with the mediator and determine their commitment to the process, they have an opportunity to discuss the various settlement processes available to them, such as interpersonal negotiations, negotiations through an advocate, therapy, litigation, and adjudication. Those parties who choose mediation have already reached their first agreement—to resolve the issues in private and in a nonadversary fashion.

Thus, many of the tasks in this stage of the mediation process are the same goals that a therapist hopes to accomplish initially—establishing trust, rapport, and commitment to the process and defining the relationship between the therapist and the clients. The therapist may foreshadow the course of therapy by describing the general treatment plan and typical resistances to change that the client or family may encounter. Although the resolution of hurt, anger, fear, guilt, and rejection is not the purpose of divorce mediation as it is the purpose of therapy, these issues are often germane to the mediation process (Folberg & Taylor, 1984).

Defining the Issues

When a mediator first asks the parties to define the issues in dispute, most parties do so by answering with their solution—or with their "final" position: "Well, the dispute is about custody—I want custody and so does he (she) " or "I think I should have the house because . . . and he (she) thinks he (she) should have the house because. . . ." This positional bargaining (Fisher & Ury, 1981; Moore, 1983) is typically a dead end; at best, it leads the parties into a contest of wills to see who can convince and/or wear down the other.

The mediator's task is now twofold: (1) to move the parties from this positional posture to a discussion of their basic needs and interests and (2) to bring to the surface any underlying conflicts that may inhibit the mediation process. The mediator typically does this through questions, such as "What is it that you are unhappy about?" and "What is it that you are really looking for?" As this questioning process proceeds, the couple begins to deal with a number of other issues, often longstanding issues, that may be related to the marital relationship or may be individual and specific to each spouse. In this way, conflicts of both a relational and a personal nature are identified.

The task of the mediator is to assist the couple in cataloging the various kinds of conflicts. Kessler (1978) offered three categories: (1) topical issues, (2) personal issues, and (3) relational issues. Topical issues may be described as the "point-at-ables" of divorce, i.e., division of property, finances, the time that the children will spend with each parent. These issues are often physical and observable, and they make up most divorce stipulations.

Personal issues are the internal conflicts and concerns that each individual brings to mediation, such as self-esteem, power, anger, or loss of love objects. These may be rooted in the individual's family of origin. Mediation often brings these longstanding personal issues out into the open. In addition, the desire to turn over a new leaf and behave differently is often observed in divorce mediation; for example, "I was never able to assert myself in the marriage, and I'm not going to let him (her) walk all over me now."

Relationship issues are the accumulated issues that were unresolved during the marriage and have remained unresolved as the couple moves through the divorce process. The hurts, the angers, the unfulfilled expectations, and the unkept promises of the marriage, which are the substance of relationship conflicts, are often at the root of disputes brought to mediation.

The mediator should recognize the legitimacy of topical, personal, and relationship conflicts, but should apprise the parties that mediation focuses on the topical issues. The goal is not the resolution of the personal and relationship issues, but rather the management of these issues as they become road blocks to the resolution of the topical issues.

The issues dealt with in therapy are different from the issues dealt with in mediation. Therapy tends to focus on personal and relationship issues rather than topical issues. Clients typically contact a therapist because they are unhappy or because they are finding it difficult to cope with a life event or relationship issue. Furthermore, a therapist often takes a greater responsibility for defining the issues than does a mediator. As a client presents the problem, the therapist is analyzing the underlying psychological roots of the problem. The therapist's analysis of the problem is based on an understanding of psychodynamics, emotional needs, systems theory, and the communication process. The therapist then presents the issue to clients and recommends a course of treatment on that basis.

The mediator, in contrast, analyzes the presenting issues from a different perspective. Although not oblivious to the psychological nature of the dispute, the mediator assists the couple in defining conflicts according to mutual needs and interests and in recognizing the need to separate psychological conflict from negotiations to resolve the topical issues. The mediator's analysis of the problem focuses on the settlement of contractual issues and the removal of road blocks to the bargaining and mediation process.

Processing the Issues

As the mediator helps the parties to focus on the topical issues of the divorce and reframe them as interests or needs, the parties begin to discuss the issues in a manner conducive to settlement rather than in the competitive push-pull manner that results from the taking of a position. The mediator can now attend to the parties' communication and negotiation processes. The communication process of most couples beginning divorce mediation reflects their behavior during the marriage. It was ineffective then and probably is ineffective now as well. Like a therapist, the mediator must demonstrate this to the couple and provide them with more effective communication tools.

The mediator may point out patterns of rhetorical conflict (expanding conflict for its own sake) that result in an impasse and contrast this with such techniques as active listening, "I" statements, paraphrasing, modeling, and role reversal. By asking one party to take the other's position, the mediator helps each to understand the other's needs and goals. Even a modicum of understanding and empathy begins to erode an adversarial, competitive relationship.

Personal and relationship issues typically block communication. For some couples, mediation has two opposing functions: it is a means of continuing the relationship while separating from the relationship. Some couples seem to relish the mediation process, but avoid reaching any agreements. This is similar to the resistance to change that many clients experience in therapy.

The mediator must attend to personal and relationship issues that become road blocks to the settlement of topical issues. Reestablishing the parties' commitment to the process of mediation and identifying the issues relevant to mediation are ways of managing the emotional climate. Acknowledging the relationship issues and asking the parties to deal with these issues so that they do not inhibit the process of mediation is another management technique used in the mediation process. Unlike the therapist, who delves into the personal and relationship conflicts, the mediator stops short of resolving these types of issues and instead tries to help the couple develop a means of managing these issues while focusing on the topical issues; the mediator tries to detour around these issues.

A mediator is often confronted with the relational issues of power and control. Power may lie with the spouse who has a verbally aggressive style, who is more articulate, or who knows more about such things as finances or child development. Rarely are parties evenly matched in all areas. Frequently, however, it is this imbalance that provides a solution to the conflict; the mediator can assist the parties in combining their assets (their power) in a cooperative decision-making process that can work to their mutual gain.

The issues of power and control may be related to family of origin, unmet psychological needs, and emotional well-being. Rather than accepting these differences between the couple, the therapist works toward an understanding of these differences and a resolution of them. Therapists must often become an advocate for a client in therapy and must then deal with the problem of triangulation. Inexperienced mediators may find themselves in the same position. More sophisticated mediators view themselves as an advocate of the settlement process and take less responsibility for the final resolution. In mediation, client advocacy is left to the parties' attorneys.

By reorienting the parties toward mutual goals and overlapping interests, the mediator moves the parties along the resolution continuum. Fisher and Ury (1981) describe this reorienting process as moving the parties from opposite ends of the negotiation table to the same side of the table so that they sit as two judges who must make a joint determination on a particular issue. In order to move the parties to the same side of the table and continue the resolution process, the mediator assists the parties in developing a list of options that might meet their identified needs and interests. This is done without evaluating any of the options. This brainstorming process reinforces the mutuality of the problem and assists the parties in separating their interests from the solutions (Fisher & Ury, 1981). It may become evident that the parties need more information to move to the resolution stage of the mediation process. Completing homework assignments, sharing information, and consulting with outside experts may be helpful.

Resolving the Issues

Once alternatives have been generated, the couple can begin the matching and mutual accommodation process required to resolve the issues. A building block process begins in which needs and interests are matched with solutions (Fisher & Ury, 1981; Moore, in press). This building block process is simplified when issues are dealt with one at a time rather than linked together so that the resolution of one issue is dependent on the resolution of another. This is not always possible in divorce mediation, however, as plans for children and financial arrangements can be dependent on each other.

Couples often reach solutions by combining proposals, reaching tentative agreements (eliminating the need for a party to make a firm commitment to something with which he or she does not yet feel comfortable) and agreeing to agree in principle. They work to fit pieces of the options together to fashion an agreement that will cover both their shared and separate interests.

As the agreement begins to take shape, the mediator helps the parties develop a plan for finalizing and implementing the agreement. This is the culmination of the mediation process. In this final stage, relying on creativity and the generation of options allows the parties to shift their focus from the desired end to the means to that end (Moore, in press). This shift breaks the deadlock that often occurs between parties who have become enmeshed in the personal and relationship issues and who have taken positions to defend their separate stakes.

The therapy process also employs a shift in focus from the end to the means. Clients come to therapy seeking relief from emotional stress and a dysfunctional relationship (the end). The means to that end differentiates therapy from mediation, however. The therapist explores the precipitating factors (the means) of psychological and relationship stress, helping clients to understand the cause of the conflict; this then allows clients to change behaviors and approaches to troublesome situations. The cognitive understanding of the problem and the ability to satisfy underlying emotional needs based on a supportive relationship with the therapist allows clients to shift from the desire (the end) for well-being and happiness to the means to that end.

CONCLUSION

Critics who state that mediation is only a whitewash of the more substantive interpersonal and psychological issues may have a point. Yet many couples do not wish to engage in a psychotherapeutic process and find that mediation satisfies their interests in reaching a settlement. The resolution of the contractual issues provides the emotional distance and clarity that many couples need to separate physically and emotionally.

The blurring between mediation and therapy is attributable to the confusion between objectives and process. The objectives of therapy are not the objectives of mediation, but they may become the tools of the mediation process. For example, diagnosis of underlying issues is helpful in the definition of the conflict. The enhancement of self-esteem, the reinforcement of autonomy, and the extinction of dysfunctional behaviors are used in the mediation process to facilitate the couple's ability to communicate and to reach an agreement.

Mediation draws on the techniques of behavioral therapy, but differs in its focus. The historical origin of disputes is explored only when doing so is necessary to avoid an impasse and to move the mediation process along. The relationship between the mediator and the client may resemble that between a therapist and a client in some elements, such as the establishment of trust, rapport, and identification, but the agreement-producing process does not rely on these elements as much as therapy does.

Mediation is an interpersonal dispute resolution process that focuses on the contractual issues of property, finances, and plans for the children. It is designed to address the future needs of the couple and their children. The resolution of past differences and the acquisition of insight into the dynamics of the conflict may occur as a result of mediation, but they are not the goal of the process. Divorce mediation typically results in a written agreement that is incorporated into a court order.

When behavioral change or emotional well-being is the predominant goal, the process is likely to be of a therapeutic nature. When the objective is to resolve the topical and contractual issues of divorce, the practice is that of mediation.

REFERENCES

Brown, D. (1982). Divorce and family mediation: History, review, future directions. *Conciliation Courts Review, 20*(2), 1–44.

Brown, E. (1976). A model of the divorce process. *Conciliation Courts Review, 14*(2), 1–11.

Coogler, O.J. (1978). *Structured mediation in divorce settlement: A handbook for marital mediators.* Lexington, MA: D.C. Heath.

Enelow, A. (1977). *Elements of psychotherapy.* New York: Oxford University Press.

Fisher, R., & Ury, W. (1981). *Getting to yes: Negotiating agreement without giving in.* Boston: Houghton Mifflin Co.

Folberg, H.J. (1983). A mediation overview: History and dimensions of practice. *Mediation Quarterly,* September, 3–13.

Folberg, H.J., & Milne, A. (Eds.) (in press). *Divorce mediation: Theory and practice.* New York: Guilford Press.

Folberg, H.J., & Taylor, A. (1984). *Mediation: A comprehensive guide to resolving conflicts without litigation.* San Francisco: Jossey-Bass.

Framo, J. (1978). The friendly divorce. *Psychology Today,* February, 77–79, 100–102.

Gulliver, P. (1979). *Disputes and negotiations: A cross cultural perspective.* New York: Academic Press.

Hunt, M., & Hunt, B. (1977). *The divorce experience.* New York: McGraw-Hill.

Kaslow, F. (1979–1980). Stages of divorce: A psychological perspective. *Villanova Law Review, 25*(4/5), 718–751.

Kessler, S. (1978). *Creative conflict resolution: Mediation.* Atlanta: National Institute for Professional Training.

Kressel, K., Lopez-Morrilas, M., Weinglass, J., & Deutsch, M. (1978). Professional intervention in divorce: A summary of the view of lawyers, psychotherapists and clergy. *Journal of Divorce,* Winter, 119–155.

Milne, A. (1981). Family self-determination: An alternative to the adversarial system in custody disputes. *Divorce mediation: Theory and practice.* Association of Family and Conciliation Courts Conference Proceedings, December 1–19. Ft. Lauderdale, FL.

Milne, A. (1982). Divorce mediation—An idea whose time has come? *Wisconsin Journal of Family Law, 2*(2), 1–10.

Milne, A. (1983). Divorce mediation: The state of the art. *Mediation Quarterly,* September, 15–31.

Milne, A. (in press). Divorce mediation: A process of self definition and self determination. In N. Jacobson & A. Gurman (Eds.), *Clinical handbook of marital therapy.* New York: Guilford.

Moore, C. (1983). *A general theory of mediation: Dynamics, strategies and moves.* Unpublished doctoral dissertation, Rutgers.

Moore, C. (in press). Obstacles to effective divorce mediation. In J. Folberg & A. Milne (Eds.), *Divorce mediation: Theory and practice.* New York: Guilford.

Olson, D. (1975). A critical overview. In A. Gurman & D. Rice (Eds.), *Couples in conflict.* New York: Jason Aronson.

Silvano, A. (1974). *American handbook of psychiatry (2nd ed.).* New York: Basic Books.

Singer, E. (1970). *Key concepts in psychotherapy (2nd ed.).* New York: Basic Books.

2. A Systems View of Divorce Intervention Strategies

Edward W. Beal

Aʟʟ ᴅɪᴠᴏʀᴄᴇs ᴀʀᴇ ɴᴏᴛ ᴛʜᴇ sᴀᴍᴇ, ʙᴜᴛ ᴀʟʟ ᴅɪᴠᴏʀᴄɪɴɢ ꜰᴀᴍɪʟɪᴇs use some societal agency in the divorce process. Furthermore, families separate according to the societal agency used in the divorce process, as well as according to the way they are organized. The relationship between the societal agency and the divorcing family parallels the organization of the spouse relationship.

Family systems theory can be used to describe not only the relationship processes of divorcing families, but also the relationship of these families to the helping systems. A cornerstone of family systems theory is the concept of emotional attachment, i.e., the mutual emotional influence that occurs between any two people who are emotionally important to one another. Family relationships reflect the management of this emotional attachment among all family members. According to family systems theory, the management depends on the intensity of the attachment and the degree of stress experienced by the individuals involved.

This paper is based on information obtained from 200 families seen in private practice and at a community mental health center over the past 7 years. The information was collected from clinical interviews of parents and children, from school reports and other supporting material, and from a standard clinical psychiatric evaluation. The length of time that couples in this study had been married ranged from a few months to more than 30 years. All the families were in the process of divorcing or had been recently divorced. Families were predominantly white. They were working middle-class residents of an urban area. The average mean age of parents was mid-30s.

PERSPECTIVE OF FAMILY SYSTEMS THEORY

Emotional Attachment

All family relationships have an emotional balance or equilibrium. Marriage and divorce are nodal events in the family life cycle that require shifts in this equilibrium because they reflect variations in the intensity of the emotional attachment among individuals. In turn, the intensity of emotional attachment reflects the integration of two broad processes that exist in all families. One process leads toward the development of individuality and emotional autonomy—that which an individual defines as important for self. The other leads toward emotional fusion and dependency between individuals—that which a family defines as important for its members. The degree of integration and balance between these two processes can be evaluated by examining the emotional attachment between spouses and between a parent and child.

Each marital relationship falls somewhere on a continuum between emotional autonomy and emotional fusion. The greater the fusion between two people, the more one person's attitudes, beliefs, and behavior are influenced by the other. The degree to which a person is emotionally influenced by others reflects the degree to which that person loses self-direction in life. If emotional fusion is extreme, the sudden death of one spouse is followed by total dysfunction in the remaining spouse over the course of a lifetime. An individual whose attachments and marriage are characterized by more emotional autonomy is likely to be able to negotiate sudden and serious losses of important family members with a minimum of stress and with a set of self-defined goals after a period of some dysfunction.

Stress and the Use of Compensatory Mechanisms

Like emotional attachment, stress affects the characteristics of family relationships. The more stress, the more intense the relationship; the more intense the relationship, the more emotional fusion and, therefore, the more emotional influencing. Whenever individuals are stressed, compensatory mechanisms reestablish the balance of emotional forces in their relationships. Acute stress may produce temporary changes in the character of family relationships, while chronic stress may produce more longlasting changes.

According to family systems theory, compensatory mechanisms that maintain the balance of emotional forces in family relationships include

- physical and emotional distance between individuals
- emotional conflict between individuals
- emotional, social, or physical dysfunction within an individual
- child focus

The mechanism of child focus is operating when the stress experienced by a parent appears in the form of great parental emotional investment in the child even if the child's circumstances do not realistically require it.

These compensatory mechanisms, which are present to some degree in all families, maintain balance and harmony in the family relationship system by readjusting the frequency and intensity of emotional contact. Families with less intense emotional attachment and a low level of stress can function well with periodic, moderate use of compensatory mechanisms, while families with more intense emotional attachment and a higher level of stress may use these mechanisms more frequently. Families with the highest degree of emotional attachment may find it necessary to use these mechanisms almost continuously in order to remain intact and functioning. Finally, families with high degrees of emotional attachment under low to moderate stress are likely to have one or more symptomatic dysfunctional members at any given time (Kerr, 1978).

Compensatory Mechanisms in Marital Relationships

The mechanisms used within the nuclear family system to regulate emotional attachments and anxiety include emotional, social, or physical dysfunction in one spouse; emotional conflict between spouses; physical and emotional distance between spouses; and child focus.

One spouse may assume a dominant position on emotionally based issues, while the other spouse assumes a more adaptive role. This pattern of interaction may function well unless the level of anxiety in the relationship becomes so high that the efforts of the adaptive spouse become ineffective and he or she becomes symptomatic. The dominant spouse may then respond to the symptomatic adaptive spouse by seeking physical or emotional distance, which may lead to divorce. For example, the anxious and depressed spouse of a goal-directed, professionally oriented individual may be referred to a mental health professional, allowing the nonsymptomatic spouse to leave the marriage with less guilt because the symptomatic spouse is in "good hands."

In another major relationship pattern in the marital dyad, both spouses assume primarily dominant positions in relation to emotionally based issues. When anxiety is introduced, marital conflict is likely to appear. If neither spouse can reduce his or her own anxiety or reactiveness, this pattern may lead to physical separation.

If both spouses assume primarily adaptive positions in relation to emotionally based issues between them, mutual action paralysis may occur, or both spouses may become symptomatic. These marriages may be characterized by chronic symptoms in both spouses or long-term marital conflict.

Significant emotional distance between spouses and emotional overinvolvement of one spouse with the children is another marital pattern. Theoretically, this pattern has the greatest potential for undermining the emotional autonomy of a child. This mechanism is often referred to as child focus, since family members deal with stress by focusing their anxiety on the child(ren) (Beal, 1979).

Epidemiological evidence shows that modern society is characterized by major disruptions of intimate human relationships and that such disruptions are often associated with chronic physiological arousal, since the body's major physiological mechanisms are controlled by the brain. Physiology is altered during arousal, and chronically altered physiology leads to major physical pathologies. Some physiological arousal is accompanied by behavior that resolves tensions and enhances intimacy. Many individuals, however, respond to arousal by seeking physical and emotional distance, which can maintain the physiological arousal and lead to greater tension in relationships.

The modern concept of disease and dysfunction has not incorporated data about social relationships because disease is not generally regarded as a relationship phenomenon. Modern medicine has failed to unite social and biological observations in a comprehensive theory of disease therapy. Certainly, divorce is a disruption of intimate social relationships, and it may be a byproduct of chronically altered physiology. Some individuals react to chronically altered physiology with physical disease processes, and others respond with disrupted relationships. The surgical approach to disease is similar to the legal approach to disrupted relationships in that both deal with relatively end stage problems, putting most emphasis on the blunt intervention rather than on the process that leads to these problems.

If the arousal is chronic or if the individual's compensatory response is chronic, the mind and body adapt to the prolonged stimulus so as to sustain a symptom in equilibrium. In divorcing families with a high level of chronic physiological and emotional arousal, the divorce process can lead to relationship substitution as a compensatory mechanism to deal with the chronic arousal. Rather than resolve tension with another in a relationship, substitution of a new spouse for the former spouse is used to resolve tension in the original relationship. Divorce and remarriage can be an example of this mechanism.

DECISION MAKING DURING THE DIVORCE PROCESS

Although information is important to the couple in both decisions, marriage and divorce are, for the most part, emotional decisions. Factors to be considered in evaluating the decision-making process of the marital couple include

- dating and courtship behavior
- length of courtship
- length of time between marriage and the birth of the first child
- degree of emotional involvement with the child
- decisions regarding discipline of the child
- degree to which the child is the emotional focus of marital disagreements
- intensity and chronicity of marital conflict or distance

Identification of these factors makes it possible to reach tentative conclusions about the decision-making patterns in the marital dyad, the events that activate the patterns, and the factors that influence the patterns (Beal, 1981).

Through family systems therapy, individuals learn to define their family's relationship patterns and the part each family member plays in establishing and maintaining these overall patterns. The focus is on helping each person to change himself or herself, rather than on encouraging family members to try to change each other. The family therapy approach emphasizes individual responsibility in decision making and deemphasizes individual responsivity or reactivity in decision making. Balance and mutuality in family relationships through the definition of individual patterns are most likely to promote intergenerational continuity and the resolution of problems in relationships.

As families develop greater anxiety or make a greater use of compensatory mechanisms, cooperation disappears, cohesiveness dissolves, and altruistic behavior vanishes. Cooperation is replaced by selfish behavior, and actions taken are often at cross-purposes. As cohesiveness dissolves, the family is divided into subgroups that play one dyad against another. This intrafamilial adversarial process can extend beyond family boundaries to include friends as well as members of the legal, mental health, and mediation professions.

Families with a dominant-dominant spousal organization are likely to develop conflictual relationships under stress and may initially seek therapy to resolve differences. If the anxiety cannot be contained, however, they may quickly move into the litigation phase. Families in which one spouse is dysfunctional often have an overt or covert agreement that the dysfunctional spouse will engage a mental health professional. The relationship between the dysfunctional spouse and the mental health professional may take on sufficient emotional significance to quiet the tension in the marital relationship. Should all parties be satisfied with this triangular relationship, the status quo may be maintained unless the dysfunctional spouse improves, at which time more pressure is placed on the apparently more functional spouse.

Marital relationships characterized by a high degree of physical or emotional distance may be most difficult to resolve through therapy unless both parties are motivated to improve the situation. These relationships are least likely to involve litigation unless the distance is associated with a high degree of animosity and polarization. If there is a mutual agreement to divorce, litigation is quite unlikely; if only one party wants the divorce, however, litigation is highly likely in order to counteract the intense negative feelings contained within the emotional distance. Families that use child focus as a compensatory mechanism are prime candidates for child custody litigation, especially if there is some dysfunction within the spouse who is most emotionally attached to the children.

Divorcing families deal with marital conflict through family therapy, mediation, and litigation. In the author's experience, family members have become more adversarial as they move from the choice of therapy to mediation to litigation as a method for dealing with intrafamilial problems. Family therapists emphasize the part each individual plays in the problem, maintaining that decision making for the marriage or divorce should be contained within the marital pair. Nevertheless, decision making and generating new options are not the primary focus of systems therapy; rather, the emotional factors and emotional influencing that interferes with decision making and the part each individual plays in the interference are the focus of the therapist. In essence, the process of family therapy deals with how individuals unite and divide their emotional selves in a multigenerational context. To the extent that individuals understand these processes, they will be more able to deal with how they unite and divide their financial selves and their children and/or generate new options.

Mediators keep the decision making within the marital pair, yet the most basic goal of mediation is to persuade each party to accept the largest concession of self the other is willing to make and/or to generate new options. Typically, court ordered mediation clients resolve support and property issues in court, using mediation services for custody and visitation issues. Private mediation usually deals with all four distributional questions—marital property, spousal support, child support, and custody—and in theory relies on self determination by clients (Folberg, 1983). However, by the time a family chooses mediation over therapy, the question generally is not if they will divorce, but how. Mediators, in contrast to family therapists, define distributional questions as financial and not as emotional in nature.

Litigation, the most highly adversarial of these three processes, gives the decision-making responsibility to an outside third party—judge, lawyer, or physician—and minimizes the responsibility of the spouses for decisions. Litigation encourages each spouse to blame the other for the problems and maximizes irresponsibility. In essence, this process fosters extreme use of compensatory mechanisms, such as spouse dysfunction, marital conflict, or child focus. Families engaged in this kind of behavior are the least cohesive and cooperative. Litigation often fosters dysfunctional family processes by its emphasis on individual rights over individual responsibilities.

As a family moves along the spectrum from therapy through mediation to litigation, a fundamental issue is the inability or unwillingness of the marital dyad to take responsibility for decisions, regardless of the issue. There is a myth that decision making is somehow dependent on information, but in each of the three stages, information mostly provides a framework for containing the family emotional process. Ultimately, the court intervenes in families that are unable to take responsibility for themselves. One of the important but seldom used functions of litigation is to contain the family process and return it to the area of family therapy or mediation.

FAMILY SYSTEMS APPROACH TO DIVORCING FAMILIES

Important emotional attachments occur within the entire network of the nuclear and extended family. Symptoms appear as distortions of emotional attachment or as imbalances in the system of family relationships. Thus, therapy requires working with the family as a unit to modify the management of relationships, attachments, and symptoms.

Family therapists begin by asking questions to identify relationship patterns in family emotional processes. Their first task is to define the dysfunction in the context of the overall family emotional system. A therapist relates to the family, but remains outside the family emotional field so that he or she can provide feedback to the family on the ways in which their interactional patterns lead to specific dysfunctions in each family member.

A frequent approach in family therapy is to try to decrease the intensity of an individual's emotional focus. For example, it may be necessary to shift the parental focus from a child to the marital relationship as such or to each spouse's relationship to his or her own family of origin. This shift can be accomplished most easily if parents can learn to view the child as an extension of the marital dyad and cease to see the family as an extension of the child, or can learn to reduce their own anxiety and concentrate more on self. Family problems are most likely to be resolved if such a shift can be achieved (Beal, 1979).

While working with families considering divorce, therapists must be aware of the possible development of emotional triangles so that they can avoid inadvertently aligning themselves with one of the marital pair or making a decision for them (Vigyikan, 1978). One spouse or the other frequently describes the relationship in such a manner that one is the victim and the other the victimizer. A therapist can easily be trapped in the role of rescuer. Although anxiety and symptoms may be temporarily decreased, no basic or fundamental change can occur in the marital dyad when the mental health professional serves as the rescuer in a "persecutor-persecuted" dyad.

Clearly, if there is to be a divorce, emotional triangles will develop. If the spouse who wants the divorce feels guilty about leaving, it is not uncommon for him or her to seek help for the other spouse. Conflict over the decision to divorce may diminish when the less functional spouse has the support of a therapist. The establishment of an important emotional relationship between the therapist and the apparently dysfunctional spouse often "resolves" the issue of guilt over abandonment so that the apparently more functional spouse can leave the marriage.

While the establishment of a triangle with the therapist may allow a couple to divorce more easily, it does not necessarily change the future relationship patterns of the individuals in the marriage. It is critical for the therapist to remain emotionally nonaligned in order to keep the conflictual issues and the decision to divorce between the couple. Overfocus on the decision to divorce or resolution of the child custody issue can encourage a couple to believe that making this decision is the only real problematic issue in their relationship. The emotional dissolution of a long-term intimate relationship is never simple, however. The therapist can use numerous issues in an attempt to decrease the intensity of the marital conflict. Whether reconciliation or divorce is the outcome, individuals can learn a great deal about themselves, enhance their own functioning, and improve the quality of their relationship by working through the marital conflicts (Beal, 1980).

While the marital dyad dissolves after divorce, the parental dyad persists. Therefore, it is important for family therapists, mediators, lawyers, and judges to keep in mind that making decisions is not equivalent to resolving the problem. As a couple moves along the spectrum of family therapy, mediation, and litigation, anxiety generally increases, and the adversarial process within the family extends beyond the family to be contained in part by society's intervention agencies. Litigation, as the greatest extrapolation of the intrafamily process into society, reflects that intervention. Practitioners from each profession involved must be aware that one of the most important functions their intervention can serve is to contain family anxiety as much as possible within the family itself. Once a family member believes that the intrafamily problem can be resolved through an extrafamily intervention, there is little possibility that any substantial change will occur within the family members themselves.

CASE EXAMPLES

The following four clinical examples highlight the family organization, the family divorce process, and the author's approach toward intervention within the family.

Case Example 1

Mr. A. was a highly motivated, upwardly mobile professional with an advanced degree. He had married a woman who was willing to support him through graduate school. Their courtship lasted approximately 1 year. During the first years of their marriage, it became apparent that the husband made most of the decisions involving the marital pair, and the wife adapted to whatever the husband wanted.

A child was born approximately 3 years after the marriage. The father developed a chronic illness secondary to an infectious process, which forced the mother to be care-giver to both her husband and their daughter. Once the father recovered, he became progressively more involved in his studies and bored with family life. Because of frequent conflicts, Mr. A. was often away from home, and Mrs. A. became tearful and depressed. This process continued so that Mr. A., in spite of his enormous sense of guilt, decided to leave the family and to divorce. Following the divorce itself, he kept fairly regular contact with his daughter.

Although the divorce process itself had been conflictual, the couple had been able to work it out through their respective lawyers. The reasons that the father sought therapy were the mother's impending remarriage, her plan to move to another area of the United States with their daughter, and the beginning dysfunction of their daughter in school. After the initial interview, it was apparent that the father was trying to make a continuous reentry into the emotional life of his daughter, that he was becoming progressively anxious about the close emotional intensity

North County Library

between his ex-wife and daughter (as well as about the fact that his ex-wife was planning to marry a man much like himself), and that his ex-wife's anxiety about this decision was leading to considerable dysfunction in his daughter. When Mr. A. attempted to talk about this with his ex-wife, she complained that he was interfering with her life.

After the initial consultation, Mr. A. was advised to contact a highly competent lawyer in the area who would evaluate the possibility that Mr. A. could bring a lawsuit to prevent the removal of his daughter from the area and the possibility that he might obtain custody. No therapy or mediation seemed appropriate unless Mr. A. clearly understood his chances of resolving the situation through litigation.

After it became clear that little could be resolved through litigation, meetings were held between Mr. A., his ex-wife, and their daughter. Initially, considerable anxiety was generated by the resurrection of the marital relationship; it became clear, however, that the lack of resolution of the prior emotional relationship contributed to the current symptoms. While the wishes of the 10-year-old child in this case were taken into consideration, it was believed that resolution would be more effective if the process focused between Mr. A. and his ex-wife. Through several sessions over a number of months, the former Mrs. A. was able to see the similarity between her new relationship and her previous one with Mr. A. She was also able to see how her anxiety about the new relationship was being transmitted to her child. Mr. A. came to be seen as a support rather than as an interference when it was clear that he would have open and appropriate access to his child following the move. The major emphasis in this process was to clarify the general interactional patterns within the family and the part each individual played. In discussing the practical details of decision making and planning, the family became more aware of the depression and guilt remaining from previously unresolved issues. Together, Mr. A. and his ex-wife were able to make very appropriate plans for contact between their child and both parents subsequent to the move. When it was clear to both parents that they each had a significant contribution to make to their daughter's welfare, they were able to stop blaming each other and began to focus on what each of them could do. After the marriage and the move, Mr. A. and his new wife visited in the home of the former Mrs. A. and her new husband; they reported that the social visit went very well. At last report, the daughter had become a very good student and had been placed in advanced courses.

The approach in this case was to contain the anxiety within the family, work on previously unresolved issues, and keep the unresolved prior marital problems from focusing on the child.

Case Example 2

Two highly competent professional individuals were very romantically attracted to each other almost from the beginning. The courtship was characterized by intense conflicts and highly romantic resolution of the conflicts. They indicated that they tended to overlook some of the conflictual aspects of the courtship. The time interval between initial dating and marriage was 5 months. This was the husband's second marriage and the wife's first marriage. Their daughter was born within 9 months of the marriage.

After marriage, the intense conflict was followed by emotional distance and increased activity in their respective professional lives. Both were rather dominating and inflexible regarding the emotionally based issues between them. Within 1 year and before the birth of their child, the parents separated. After the birth of the child, the marital conflict quickly focused on the well-being of the child. The parents each invited their extended families to move into their respective homes to help with the care of the newborn. When it became obvious that no compromise was possible, the parents each hired a different child psychiatrist to testify to their adequacy as a parent.

When asked to evaluate the mother-child relationship, I agreed to do so if both parties would be involved or if the husband would indicate directly to me that he refused to be involved. The initial presentation to the court was simply an appropriate visitation schedule for a very young child. Possibly because of the highly explosive nature of the spousal relationship or the judge's own personal preferences, no consideration was given to expert testimony in this court proceeding. Through their lawyers, the spouses agreed to accept another child psychiatrist as mediator regarding the appropriate visitation between the parents and the child. The child psychiatrist was unable to keep the adversarial process appropriately focused between the parents, however, and this therapeutic process quickly disintegrated.

The ensuing visitation schedule did not take into account the developmental stage of the child. The child began having significant symptoms related to the constant shifting back and forth between parents. Several months later, the mother contacted me to evaluate the symptomatology of the child and asked me if I would testify as to the effects of the visitation on the child.

I agreed to see the child, the mother, and the maternal grandmother over a period of time to study the situation. The father refused to be involved. Although information obtained this way has a built-in bias, it became apparent that the inability of the parents to cooperate was significantly contributing to the child's symptoms and that the recent suicide of the father's older sister and the previous death of one of the father's younger siblings as a result of chronic illness was fostering the child-focused process from the paternal side of the family. In general, I advised conciliation and accommodation between the parents in this process.

The mother's new efforts at compromise contrasted with the previous organization of the marital dyad in which conflict and inflexibility reigned. The father was frequently taking the mother to court on issues unrelated to the issue of visitation. The author suggested that the mother hire a new lawyer with a highly adversarial reputation. The nature of this intervention strategy paralleled the organization of the original marital dyad. Without filing any further motions, this new lawyer "persuaded" the father to cease his frequent visits to court. As the mother began to see that she could not win this case, but could reduce the harassment through the efforts of her new lawyer, she was able to take a position with the child in support of the importance of the child seeing the father, even though she was unhappy about it and did not agree with it. Relatively quickly, the child's symptomatology regarding separation anxiety improved.

Although an adversarial process is not generally recommended for the resolution of these problems, it is becoming increasingly apparent that, in highly conflictual marriages with a significant focus on blame, the court system may be used to contain the intrafamily process so that it can be worked on in therapy or mediation.

Case Example 3

In another family, the two spouses assumed primarily adaptive positions in relation to emotionally based issues between them. The father was the oldest of 10 children; the mother, the older of 2 sisters. In the father's family, his father made all the decisions and his mother complied. In the mother's family, her mother assumed a very protective role toward the children, and no overt conflict ever seemed to appear between her parents.

These two individuals dated in college, "fell in love," and became the best of friends. During the first 6 years of their marriage, they began to have some sexual difficulties, "discovered" they had nothing in common, and developed significant emotional distance between them. They considered separation, but stayed together. They decided to separate, but changed their minds. As the relationship evolved, it became apparent that they had difficulty in differing from one another.

A child was born approximately 6 years after the marriage, and parents often find it difficult to adapt their solidified relationship to parenthood when their first child is born more than 5 years after their marriage. After the birth of this child, both parents continued to work, having hired someone to take care of the child. The father indicated that he knew the relationship would eventually end because there was no flexibility in negotiating differences. He said that he would feel so guilty about initiating a separation that either he would have to desert his wife in order to avoid further contact or he would have to promote an affair by her in order for her to leave him. The mother indicated that she thought it was all right for the father to have an affair to deal with their marital problems as long as he did not tell her about it.

When the child reached approximately 4½ years of age, the parents decided that there was no future in the marriage and they would separate. The mother decided to let the father have the child because the child liked the father best. The mother characteristically had not discussed this or other issues with her extended family; after she did, her family was so upset that she changed her mind about giving up the child.

Although there was no open conflict, the couple contacted me about the best plans for the child. With little difficulty, they outlined the type of structure the child needed and the appropriate visitation and residential circumstances. They agreed to joint custody, equal time with the child, no alimony or child support, and an equal division of additional costs incurred in raising the child. It was clear that they found it easier to make decisions as parents than as spouses. Although this couple attended several sessions, worked hard, and had no overt conflictual issues, their mutual adaptiveness presented a long-term problem for them. Although they had made appropriate arrangements for the child, the couple had still not resolved the question of what would happen should one of them remarry or if one of them moved away from the area and wanted to take the child with them. They were unable to discuss this problem.

Two years later, the couple contacted me again. The mother had remarried, the father was going to remarry, and the mother's new husband was being transferred to another city. The mother planned to take the child with her. They wanted me to advise them as to what they should do about the child. A significant consideration in cases like this is which parent would do the best without the child. The mother indicated that she thought she needed the child more than the child needed her. The father indicated that he could probably function better without the child than would the mother. As a part of the decision-making process, I helped the couple to decide on a visitation schedule, but not to decide who would be the primary custodian.

This family had turned an initial strength into a liability; their adaptability to one another had led to an inability to make decisions. After several sessions, it became apparent that neither would compromise on this matter, so the father engaged a child psychiatrist to see both individuals. After an evaluation, this expert decided in favor of the father; the mother then engaged her own child psychiatrist, who subsequently decided in favor of the mother.

The child probably would have done well with either parent. A decision by an outside expert is only a decision; it does not resolve the basic paralysis between the parents.

Case Example 4

Initially, Mr. and Mrs. D. were very emotionally and sexually attracted to one another. During the 3 years prior to their marriage, they had lived together for varying periods of time. Mrs. D. described her husband as the "knight in shining armor who will take care of me the rest of my life." Mr. D. thought his wife looked like a famous movie actress.

Although there was an intense emotional attachment between these two people, they were unable to commit themselves to marriage. Mr. D.'s mother was divorced when he was approximately 2 years old and was subsequently married and divorced four times. Mrs. D.'s extended family was primarily intact and, although geographically distant from them, she remained very closely tied to them emotionally. Because of the intensity of the relationship and the difficulty of the commitment, Mr. D. moved out of the apartment the couple was sharing. Shortly thereafter, Mrs. D. became aware that she was pregnant, and the couple married 2 months later as a result.

The husband had agreed to the marriage because of the pregnancy, but he did not inform anyone in his extended family or in his office that his wife was pregnant. He moved in and out of the house several times before the birth of the child, complaining that his wife's emotional attachment had shifted from him to a focus on her pregnancy and the new baby and that he had felt quite left out. As Mr. D. removed himself from this intense relationship between mother and baby, however, his wife's anxiety significantly increased.

At the time of the birth, Mr. D. had left the home, and his wife became quite depressed. Within a few months, her functioning began to improve, and she rather frequently called her husband to discuss the health of their newborn baby. Mr. D. agreed to return during the evenings and weekends in order to help his wife with the initial care of their child. During these visits, Mrs. D. would offer a variety of excuses to keep her husband around the house longer. She finally proposed that they live in the house together as brother and sister rather than as man and wife.

Mr. and Mrs. D. continued to see each other a great deal, but also continued to have great difficulty committing themselves to the relationship. Within a short period of time, an intense conflictual relationship developed, and Mr. D. again moved out of the house. Mrs. D. responded initially by pretending to be ill, then becoming depressed, and then calling one day to say someone broke into her house and raped her, all of which was followed by a suicide attempt.

During these interactions, in which Mrs. D. used her child to get her husband back, there was a significant decrease in her own functioning. The husband's focus of concern shifted from his wife's well-being to that of their child. While his wife was hospitalized for her suicide attempt, he sought custody of their daughter and later went to court to obtain legal custody. The mother's hospital psychiatrist discharged her the next day, indicating that this episode was just an attempt to get her husband back. Believing that his wife should not be allowed to have the child because she was mentally disturbed, Mr. D. demanded an independent psychiatric evaluation.

During the next year, this couple went to court on approximately seven different occasions. At one time, the father was awarded custody; at another time, the judge decreed joint custody, giving the child to the father one-third of the time and to the mother two-thirds of the time. At least four different psychiatrists were involved. Two testified on each side, and one psychiatrist reviewed just the psychiatric documents on the individuals without interviewing the parents. The court also hired its own caseworkers to evaluate the family circumstances.

At some level, both parents realized this process was nonsensical and agreed, at the suggestion of the wife's lawyer, to participate in mediation. Both parents agreed that the father was capable of giving good physical, custodial care to the 2-year-old child, but that the father would function better emotionally than the mother without the child. Over a series of weeks, the mediation sessions were periodically interrupted by ongoing litigation. The couple made a serious attempt to resolve the custody issues through mediation; however, both believed they had a 100% chance of winning through litigation, and neither was willing to make a substantial compromise in mediation.

After a year in the court system, a final decision was made—custody was awarded to the mother. The father vowed to take the case to the state's supreme court, questioning the "tender years" presumption in which custody of a young female child is awarded to the mother. At this point, the father was transferred by his employer to a distant city. Agreement had been reached regarding visitation, but the father refused to return the child after the first visitation. He went to court in the new jurisdiction and reopened the entire issue, stating that there was significant evidence of the mother's instability and that returning the child to the mother would be psychologically harmful to the child. The Uniform Child Custody Act had not been adopted in this jurisdiction, and an attorney was appointed for the child.

The attorney for the child believed that the evidence had to be reviewed. Although he talked with the mother's original attorney, the mediator, and the other psychiatrists originally involved in the case and felt satisfied that the mother was not physically or psychologically abusive, he insisted that the mother fly across the country for a psychiatric reevaluation. The mother seriously considered dropping litigation and allowing the father to keep the child. After considerable debate, she decided to participate in the evaluation. After the evaluation and another court hearing, the mother once again was awarded custody of the child. It was later reported that the father had been apprehended at an international airport, attempting to take the child to a foreign country. Further communication indicated that the mother had taken the child, returned home to her extended family, and filed for bankruptcy.

This case shows that the intensity of the problem between the parents can become so great that the process cannot always be contained within the family and shifts outside to the court system. Through the numerous appeals, even the court system within one state was not able to contain the problem, and it became a battle for jurisdiction between states. The second court system, in spite of having received appropriate information from the professionals associated with the first court system, defined the issue as a jurisdictional problem rather than a case to determine the best interest of the child.

Clearly, mediation efforts are unlikely to be successful if a family member believes that he or she may "win" through litigation or if litigation cannot be used to contain the process within the family. When a family is organized around intensity and inability to assume responsibility, a decision imposed on the family, whatever it may be, is almost irrelevant.

CONCLUSION

The emotional attachments established in marriage are resolved to some extent in many divorces, but they are completely resolved in very few divorces. In spite of legal and social resolutions of the relationship, emotional attachment between former spouses often persists. The parental relationship continues. The degree to which children and parents can maintain balanced interpersonal functioning and the extent to which a family systems perspective can help them require much more research than they have received to date. The family's emotional equilibrium and organization prior to divorce significantly contribute to the functioning of children and the parents during and following the divorce process. They also give many clues to the ways in which family members will make use of societal agencies to resolve or not to resolve problems during the divorce process.

REFERENCES

Beal, E. (1979). Children of divorce: A family systems perspective. *Journal of Social Issues, 35*(4).

Beal, E. (1980). Separation, divorce and single-parent families. In E. Carter & M. McGoldrick (Eds.), *The family life cycle: A framework for family therapy.* New York: Gardner Press.

Beal, E. (1981). Family systems theory and child custody determinations. In A. Gurman (Ed.), *Questions and answers in the practice of family therapy.* New York: Brunner/Mazel.

Folberg, J. (1983). A mediation overview: History and dimensions of practice. *Mediation Quarterly, 1.*

Kerr, M. (1978). Emotional factors in the onset and course of cancer. In R.R. Sagar (Ed.), *Georgetown Family Symposia,* Vol. IV, Washington, DC.

Vigyikan, P.D. (1978). *Triangles.* Philadelphia: Dorrance and Company.

3. Mediation at Different Stages of the Divorce Process

Sarah Childs Grebe

MEDIATION HAS BEEN USED TO RESOLVE VARIOUS TYPES OF CONFLICT for thousands of years in numerous cultures (D.G. Brown, 1982). Mediation for issues related to separation and divorce is still quite new, however. Coogler, who founded the Family Mediation Association in 1974 to promote mediation for separation and divorce, is generally considered the father of the movement. Coogler (1978) emphasized that mediators must be knowledgeable in the underlying processes for the disputes they mediate.

Separation and divorce mediation is particularly complex because there are many different aspects. For mediation of co-parenting issues, the mediator must be knowledgeable about child development to help parents make appropriate decisions about their children. For property division, the mediator must be aware of legal questions and techniques to evaluate businesses or pensions so that the division is truly equitable. For resolution of support (spousal and child), the mediator must know budgeting techniques, contingencies in the law, and tax issues. Underlying all these complicated factual areas are issues arising from the effects of what has been termed the divorce process on a divorcing couple.

Mediators should understand what their clients are experiencing emotionally, but should refuse to allow these emotional aspects to cloud the mediation issues at hand. In many instances, the resolution process is blocked by the emotional aspects. Experienced mediators are able to use their knowledge of the divorce process to determine which couples will be helped by mediation, as well as where and how emotional stumbling blocks will be manifested in ongoing cases. They can use this assessment to keep the mediation process on track, avoid crossing the boundary into therapy, and circumvent possible impasses.

Several authors have described divorce as a process that occurs over time rather than a distinct event (Bohannon, 1971; E.M. Brown, 1976a, 1976b; Ibrahim, 1984; Kaslow, 1981; Kessler, 1975). Most of these authors have postulated that a divorcing person goes through a number of stages. These stages can be delineated fairly clearly. There seems to be agreement that not all persons go through all stages in their entirety or with the same intensity (E.M. Brown, 1976b; Kaslow, 1981). According to most authors, the phases and stages of divorce generally progress in a linear fashion, although there may be a recycling through some emotional states (E.M. Brown, 1976b) and stages (Ibrahim, 1984).

STATIONS OF DIVORCE

Bohannon (1971) described six stations of divorce: (1) emotional, (2) legal, (3) economic, (4) co-parental, (5) community, and (6) psychic.

Instead of outlining stages in a linear fashion, Bohannon set out distinct segments or tasks that must be completed by a person experiencing divorce. Only the emotional and psychic aspects of his schema seem to be actual stages. According to Bohannon, the emotional divorce is the first aspect experienced and psychic divorce the last. Completion of these six stations may or may not be concurrent. Bohannon further described the tasks and the emotional states underlying each of the six stations as follows:

1. emotional divorce. The couple must deal with the deteriorating marriage. The spouses feel hurt, angry, and unable to share their feelings with each other constructively.
2. legal divorce. This specifically creates remarriageability. The spouses may feel bewildered, as if they have lost control.
3. economic divorce. The couple must deal with the details of the property settlement. Each spouse may feel cheated by the other and by circumstances.
4. co-parental divorce. The issues of custody, visitation, and the single-parent home must be resolved. The spouses feel guilty about depriving their children of a two-parent home.
5. community divorce. The couple must often deal with changes in friends and community. The spouses feel anger at the situation and each other; they also feel despair at the infidelity of friendships.
6. psychic divorce. Each spouse must become autonomous. This is usually the most difficult and most scary aspect of divorce. Each spouse feels very afraid and lonely.

Bohannon's schema is very useful in helping mediation clients to identify the tasks of divorce and to understand the cause of certain feelings. For some people, being able to say "That's why I feel that way " or "I'm not the only one in this boat " is very therapeutic. In addition, a mediator can use the six stations to pinpoint possible blocks to the mediation process. Some clients can tell the mediator the reasons for their reactions; others are not so in touch with the underlying emotional components of their responses. By pinpointing the possible area of difficulty, the mediator can attempt to remove the block so that mediation can proceed constructively.

For example, the person who acts hurt and angry, and who finds it impossible to speak of the spouse without a derogatory statement, has not fully accepted the deterioration of the marriage and his or her own responsibility for it. This person is still processing the emotional divorce. In mediation, this person might be unable to focus on any task that might bring the marriage closer to dissolution, at the same time zinging the spouse with nasty verbal barbs. Each attempt by the mediator to focus the discussion may end with a "Yeah, but" statement by the "resistant" spouses, leading into a tirade against the other spouse. The mediator's task here is twofold: to stop such attacks and to eliminate the person's need to make such attacks. This might be achieved simply by labeling the reason for these zingers and demonstrating their effect on mediation, by holding a short exploration and blowing-off steam session, or by recommending concurrent counseling (by someone other than the mediator) to help the person come to grips with the situation.

A spouse who wants a speedy divorce may try to rush through the process and terminate any involvement with the current spouse as quickly as possible. This person is likely to resist the process of gathering the necessary information. The difference is in the attitude. This person wants to come to an agreement posthaste. Often, the legal divorce is being sought so that the person can marry someone else. He or she is not blocking the resolution as much as avoiding a thorough examination of the consequences. This person also wants the mediator to provide parameters for the decisions that must be made, such as what the court generally sets as child support for a person with a certain income and what is a typical mediated visitation arrangement. Control is sought through quick resolution. The mediator must slow down the process and resist agreements that have not been well thought out by both spouses.

If one spouse feels cheated by the situation or by the other spouse, it may be manifested in the economic divorce. In order to punish the "bad" spouse for the disruption of the marriage, the "cheated" spouse may try to obtain more than an equitable amount of the property or may demand more spousal support for a longer time than is necessary to secure financial independence and a decent life style. Spouses can appear to be very amicable with each other during mediation sessions, but if this area is very difficult to resolve, the underlying emotional aspects of the economic divorce bear exploration.

Parents often feel guilty about the disruption their divorce is causing in their children's lives. Many have heard that there must be one primary care-giver (Goldstein, Freud, & Solnit, 1973) to avoid causing the child(ren) untold emotional trauma, or they have heard that the child(ren) must have both parents for healthy emotional development (Wallerstein & Kelly, 1980). Sometimes, their uncertainty takes the form of attempts to severely limit the amount of time the other parent spends with the children. Other parents err in the other direction, setting up schedules that are impossible for anybody to keep, given their other obligations. A mediator must insist that parents consider all the consequences of their actions and decisions about their children. Ultimately, however, they must make a decision that they can both support. If the parents are not happy with the arrangements, their children will not be happy either. It is very tempting for parents who feel guilty to leave the decisions to their children in an attempt to make up for "this terrible thing we are doing to them." If this happens, the co-parental divorce will not be resolved.

Community divorce may present itself in mediation when the spouses must decide such questions as who retains the pool membership or who stays in the house (when there is no overriding reason for a certain decision). More often, it arises when one or both spouses suddenly change their minds on a question that had already been resolved. The spouse who is changing his or her mind has usually been discussing the situation with friends or relatives who have offered different solutions. It is difficult for these people not to take sides during the divorce process. To be helpful and demonstrate their loyalty, they feel they must ensure that their friend obtains everything possible in the settlement. If the divorcing person is especially bitter or angry, these "helpful" friends are particularly hard to resist. The mediator must deflect these inputs and help the spouse not only to make his or her own decisions, but also to deal with the reaction of the other spouse, who may feel abandoned by former friends.

When spouses have not lived on their own for many years, the psychic divorce can be very difficult. Both may realize that their relationship is no longer viable, yet they cling to it as a haven in an unfriendly world. If a couple have not separated when they come for mediation, separation may become an issue for mediation. For some couples, it is the only issue they can deal with until it actually occurs. Spouses in this situation frequently find it very difficult to locate an apartment that they like or can afford, or to determine which household furnishings to take with them—anything to delay the inevitable. Usually, the mediator's gentle insistence on completion of the assigned tasks, such as reading the rental section of the newspaper or listing the house contents and discussing them in a session, moves mediation clients through a mild case of separation anxiety. When the underlying problem is more severe, as in a highly enmeshed couple, mediation itself may be inappropriate (Kressel, Jaffee, Tuchman, Watson, & Deutsch, 1980), or concurrent therapy may be necessary.

STAGES OF DIVORCE

Some authors (Froiland & Hozman, 1977; Ibrahim, 1984; Weisman, 1975) have compared the stages of divorce to the stages of dying set forth by Kubler-Ross (1969):

1. denial and isolation
2. anger
3. bargaining
4. depression
5. acceptance

Froiland and Hozman (1977) followed Kubler-Ross almost exactly. Weisman (1975) placed depression before anger and substituted reorientation of life style and identity for bargaining. Ibrahim (1984) expanded the basic 5 stages of Kubler-Ross to 10; he added threat, separation, shock (because of legal action), and new start and separated isolation-withdrawal from denial.

Ibrahim's schema suffers from the problem that haunts all the stage theories of divorce. He attempted to define in a linear fashion distinct units of a process that is not really linear. In addition, he appeared to emphasize the negative reactions of spouses going through divorce without any consideration of the possible positive outcomes. For example, he stated that the acceptance phase can be summarized by the statement "I wish you luck, but I hope you will never make it" (p. 86). In order to mediate a dispute successfully, the mediator must emphasize the first part of such a statement and downplay the second. A sociologist, Ibrahim also made assertions such as "Seeking marriage counseling is another form of denying that divorce is imminent" (p. 84). Some of the concepts he discussed, such as inward and outward anger, superstitious bargaining, and reactive and preparatory depression, can be useful to the mediator attempting to assess the emotional climate for a particular couple.

The Kessler Model

Kessler (1975) used a different set of labels for the seven stages described in her schema:

1. disillusionment
2. erosion
3. detachment
4. physical separation
5. mourning
6. second adolescence
7. hard work

Spouses are unlikely to seek mediation for separation and divorce while in the disillusionment stage. Therefore, the stages of interest to a mediator follow the first stage. Once the spouses have moved into the erosion stage and begun to manifest their disappointment and dissatisfaction in increasingly destructive ways, the stage is set, so to speak, for divorce. The spouse who begins to experience more and more detachment is likely to investigate possibilities, including mediation, for ending the relationship.

If a couple have been in the erosion stage for a long time before they seek mediation, they may have built up a great deal of anger, resentment, and blaming. The spouse who still hopes to elicit some kind of reaction from the other, more detached spouse may feel a particular need to express this hurt and anger overtly in the mediation sessions. If the other spouse needs to retaliate, the mediator may have a full-blown battle to deal with and will need a firm hand to keep the conflict in check.

If both spouses have reached the detachment stage, they are more likely to utilize mediation in a constructive way throughout the sessions. They will be able to follow the mediator's instructions to put emotions aside, because neither has much interest in continuing the marriage. In addition, they may want to settle things fairly quickly so that one or the other can move out by a certain date. As long as such deadlines are not motivated by the desire to avoid responsibility, they can be very effective in keeping mediation on track.

The ideal couple for mediation is one in which the spouses have been separated for 6 months to 1 year and thus are into Kessler's fourth stage: physical separation. When spouses are physically separated for some period of time before coming to mediation, both may have achieved a certain level of acceptance and are willing to formalize the fait accompli. Not all couples in this situation sail through mediation without any problems, however. Some do, but many do not.

Sometimes, one spouse is completely thrown by the separation. The fifth stage, mourning, is very difficult for this spouse. It is as if one spouse stays in the stage of mourning, while the other skips to the stage of second adolescence. They are polarized in this phase of their relationship as they probably were in their marital relationship. When this happens, mediation can become a series of starts and stops because the depressed spouse is likely to assume the outcome for him or her will be negative, and the "manic" spouse becomes very hard to pin down.

When both spouses realize what is involved in living separate lives, they have reached the stage of hard work. They are more willing to put the time and energy into gathering the information for a settlement based on fact rather than conjecture. They can see more possibilities for life apart from each other and are ready to move on to a new life.

The Kaslow Model

Kaslow (1981) reviewed many of these theories of divorce and maintained that none differentiates feelings, behaviors, and tasks to be accomplished. To this end, she proposed a dialectic model of the stages of divorce. This model seems to be both an expansion and a combination of the tasks from Bohannon's six stations and the emotional experiences delineated in Kessler's seven stages. Kaslow outlined three stages of divorce: (1) predivorce: deliberation period; (2) during divorce: litigation period; and (3) postdivorce: reequilibration period. Each of these three stages has two different sets of feelings, which in turn have what Kaslow called requisite actions and tasks.

Some of Kaslow's model, such as the during divorce stage, is applicable only to the traditional adversarial divorce. For couples who go through private mediation, this is merely a formality, since they determine most aspects of their settlement prior to filing for divorce. In addition, many of the tasks (e.g., stabilization of a new life style) seen as part of the third stage are accomplished for many couples during the mediation process, and many of the feelings (e.g., resignation and acceptance) have been experienced as well.

Kaslow emphasized that the stages do not occur in invariant sequence. This is evident from a comparison of the placement of the various emotional components in the different theories. For instance, there is agreement that depression occurs somewhere in the divorce process, but not just where in the sequence it belongs. Some couples reconcile, others skip certain stages, and still others return to earlier stages. Some couples cycle through once or several times and move on, others becomed bogged down and do not move on. According to Kaslow, the latter couples are the ones who linger in anger, self-pity, and despair. They are also the ones who return to court again and again, seeking a judicial solution to an emotional problem. The mediator frequently has a very difficult time getting them to move forward without concurrent therapy. Such a bogged down couple is unlikely to come for mediation voluntarily, however.

It is more likely that a couple will seek mediation when only one spouse appears mired in an earlier stage. If a couple with two such mired members does appear or is ordered for mediation, the spouses often attempt to turn the mediation into a free-for-all or something more akin to a therapy session.

The mediator must resist the temptation to follow this agenda (an especially seducing one for the mediator with a therapist background). Allowing the sessions to become more like therapy on a regular basis generally backfires. The spouse who has the clearer understanding of mediation and its purpose will lose his or her confidence in the mediator's ability to keep the sessions focused and on target. If the couple have had some experience with therapy, they may need specific guidelines as to the difference. One spouse may welcome the crossing of the boundaries as a diversion; the other may see it as a serious breach of the mediation contract. The mediator who can see no tasks being completed and no issues being settled needs to determine whether the couple is ready for mediation and whether their goals are confused—therapy or resolution.

The Brown Model: Initiation vs. Noninitiation

E.M. Brown (1976a, 1976b) postulated a two-stage divorce process: (1) the decision-making phase and (2) the restructuring phase. Both Brown (1976a) and Kaslow (1981) postulated a 2- to 3-year period for the completion of the divorce process. According to Brown (1976b), the first stage takes about 12 months and the restructuring phase about 24 months. Furthermore, the decision-making phase in which divorce is first discussed as an option usually follows a long period of marital conflict and stress. It would encompass the first three stages described by Kessler (1975), the first stage described by Kaslow (1981), and the first station described by Bohannon (1971).

Brown's second phase begins once the decision to divorce has been made. It involves the couple's decision to separate physically. In order to do so, they must experience five major subprocesses: (1) legal, (2) social, (3) economic, (4) parent-child, and (5) emotional. These subprocesses are very similar to Bohannon's six stations of divorce. I have, however, equated Bohannon's emotional divorce with Brown's first stage of decision making, not her emotional subprocess.

Brown pointed out that her two-phase schema applies to the individual, not the couple. Because a mediator works with both spouses and because it is rare for two members of a couple to be completely synchronized in their decision to separate and/or divorce, an assessment of the couple's appropriateness for mediation must take into account the stage at which each member of that couple is in the divorce process. From her work with couples in divorce therapy, Brown (1976b) devised a model of the emotional process of divorce that is based on the concept of an initiator and a noninitiator of the divorce. This is not used to determine who is to blame, but to determine how to work with each person and the couple and the disparity in their actions and emotions as a result of their being out of phase.

The spouse who actually initiates the divorce process has generally completed certain emotional tasks. He or she has been through the most painful part and done the hardest work, often before the other spouse is consciously aware that a decision to divorce is pending. The initiator may have already "worked through" the sense of failure and disillusionment, as well as the feelings of loss and anger, and arrived at a tentative decision to separate. He or she then presents this decision to the spouse, who usually reacts in a manner that does not encourage reconciliation, even though this may be the one thing most desired. The noninitiator not only must face all the same emotional work the initiator may have already completed, but also feels betrayed and left out of this major decision by the initiator. In addition, the noninitiator may have to deal with the reality of physical separation while still in emotional shock. Noninitiators often say, "If he'd told me what he was thinking, I would have suggested counseling (or some other possibility) " or "It's her decision. I'll go through mediation, but why should I pay for her divorce? She has to pay all the costs." The latter sentiment is often expressed by spouses who feel the need to avoid responsibility for the breakup of the marriage. This, as well as the need to maintain control over one's life, is behind many contested divorces (E.M. Brown, 1976a).

Spouses may inquire about divorce mediation before either one has made a firm decision to separate or divorce. In this instance, the mediator explores with the couple several possibilities or options. One of these options is a marriage assessment (see "Marital Assessment as an Option in Divorce Mediation" in this volume) to help the spouses determine their best course. Other options include marriage counseling that may lead to reconciliation or divorce counseling that may help the couple come to terms with the dissolution, followed by mediation. The mediator who is a therapist must be very careful not to take the couple into therapy with the idea that if therapy is unsuccessful, he or she can then take the couple into mediation. Not only will the couple be confused by the therapist's "change of hats," but the therapist may be tempted to give up too soon if the option of switching to mediation is available.

Even if the decision to divorce is not firm, the mediator needs to determine who is the initiator. In some cases, the initiator is actually closer to a decision than he or she admits and has not said so for fear of creating problems with the spouse. Through a limited discussion of whose idea it was to investigate their different options, the spouses can often clarify their positions on reconciliation. This allows the initiator to break the news gently to his or her spouse, sometimes confirming the noninitiator's suspicions. Such revelations often bring a sense of relief to both spouses. The decision is now out in the open and available for discussion. Couples in this situation often ask if the separation, as well as the other areas under consideration, can be mediated. While the questions of whether to separate and whether to divorce are not appropriate decisions for mediation, the details of *how* and *when* definitely are.

Spouses who seek mediation for a "trial" separation may be approached in a similar vein. Again, it is important to determine if the true initiator is trying to break the news of divorce gently. Some people think that it will be easier to reach agreement on a trial separation, although they have no intention of reconciling. Two things are crucial in the negotiations to mediate a trial separation: (1) the spouses should agree to mediate as if this were a permanent separation to avoid making ill-advised concessions on the theory that they are short-term concessions, and (2) the spouses should understand that holding out false hope of reconciliation will actually jeopardize the mediation in the long run. When the noninitiator realizes that the initiator had no thought of reconciliation, the noninitiator may lose trust in the agreements on the ground that they were reached under those false pretenses. Furthermore, some noninitiators cannot cooperate with the mediation process unless they understand that the initiator really means to terminate their relationship, using the adversarial route if necessary.

Brown (1976a) listed a number of factors for a counselor to consider when determining whether separating spouses are ready to make a decision to divorce. A mediator can also use these guidelines to assess appropriateness of mediation and to determine where emotional blocks to progress are likely to occur once mediation has begun. One indication of an individual's readiness to decide is his or her willingness to take responsibility for the decision. If the initiator continues to blame the noninitiator for their marital problems or exhibits unabating anger against the noninitiator, he or she still has a strong emotional attachment to the spouse. Mediation in this instance can be very difficult. Highly enmeshed couples who are highly ambivalent or very embittered often do not utilize mediation effectively (Kressel et al., 1980). Most mediation failures probably occur when spouses are unwilling to accept their part in the divorce.

The expression of anger in mediation, in itself, is not counterproductive, nor is it an indication that mediation is inappropriate. In most cases, anger can be dealt with effectively in mediation; it can also be very therapeutic, whether expressed by the initiator or the noninitiator. The key is to limit and to manage the anger (E.M. Brown, 1976b). The initiator who continues to blame the other spouse is attempting to shift the perceived power in the relationship and get the counselor to punish the other spouse. The mediator must be particularly aware of such moves and avoid either colluding with the initiator or protecting the noninitiator.

The actual physical separation begins the restructuring phase for the couple (E.M. Brown, 1976a, 1976b). Because the noninitiator often begins the most difficult emotional tasks at separation, this person may be experiencing extreme overload at this time. The crisis facing couples who are just about to separate or who have just separated may be more severe than the crises that occur at any other time in the divorce process. The anger, frustration, and fear for the future have often burst full-blown through the denial of the noninitiator. Both spouses must cope with the daily details of the new situation. The initiator is ready to move on, while the noninitiator may just feel lost and unable to move at all.

The noninitiator may see mediation either as a stabilizing force or as just one more complication in life. Noninitiators who take the first position do not necessarily sail through mediation, but they see the benefits and try to be truly cooperative. On the other hand, spouses who are totally overwhelmed by the surrounding events may need some time to sort out what has happened and come to terms with the separation before they can accept mediation. Sometimes, a noninitiator requests a delay for this purpose. If the mediator senses that it is not a tactic to avoid the inevitable, he or she may support such a delay. The initiator must be willing to support it as well, however, or he or she will seek another way to resolve the marital situation.

Couples who have been separated several months to a year are better candidates for mediation than those who have very recently separated. Both the initiator and the noninitiator have handled daily activities apart from each other. They may even have experimented with various living arrangements for their children. In addition, unless one of them has gotten stuck in an earlier stage and is still heavily blaming the other, both spouses have usually completed many of the emotional tasks surrounding separation.

OTHER CONSIDERATIONS

When couples have been separated more than 1 or 1½ years without any formal arrangements between them, it is important to the success of the mediation to find out why. Many couples in this situation have religious reasons for not seeking a divorce, and they may see mediation as helping them to commit a sin. Groups such as Separated and Divorced Catholics can help these couples come to terms with the religious and emotional aspects of their divorce, while the mediator helps them with the practical aspects.

If religion is not the stumbling block to resolution, the couple may have been unable to handle the restructuring phase. E.M. Brown's model (1976b) shows that marriage remains the couple's primary reference point right after the separation. One of the tasks for the noninitiator is to acknowledge the fact of the separation. Couples who have been separated for years, but have not divorced, are usually caught in this phase. When one or both spouses are able to move beyond this point, they may find it difficult to negotiate arrangements different from those that have evolved over time. The person receiving support, for example, may be reluctant to take a lower amount than has been received in the past, even though it makes sense financially in view of both adults' situations. On the other hand, the payer may be unwilling to pay more, even though that also makes sense financially. Even minor adjustments can be difficult for this couple. The mediator does not have to deal with the spouses' inability to live separately so much as with their inability to part emotionally. Often, one of them will make this move only if a new relationship is being formed, providing the impetus for changing the old one.

The divorce mediator may encounter other extremes in practice, such as the abuser and the coerced noninitiator. Mediation for abuse itself is being offered through community justice services around the United States with varying success (Bethel & Singer, 1982) and much criticism. The criticisms are primarily that the abused spouse (usually the wife) has no power in the situation and that violence cannot be mediated (Hollingsworth, 1984). When a couple seeking mediation for separation and divorce includes an abusive spouse, the mediator must decide whether mediation is appropriate, based on the issue of relative power, not violence. Most couples have an unequal balance of power, and empowering people during the mediation is one of the mediator's tasks. This may be impossible if physical abuse is involved. Sometimes, physical separation paves the way for productive mediation on the other issues; other times, it does not result in further mediation, and the couple is dissatisfied with the outcome. Mediation resulting only in physical separation may actually be a success of sorts, however, because it decreases the opportunity for abuse. Nevertheless, concerns about the use of mediation in cases involving spouse abuse are valid and need further exploration.

The coerced initiator is someone who finally says, "You've gone too far this time. I'm fed up; I'm getting a divorce." In this instance, the person who appears to be the initiator really is not. By engaging in behavior such as alcoholic binges, abuse, and affairs, one spouse may force the other spouse into the role of initiator. In these situations, there are questions about whether mediation is appropriate.

The majority of couples who come to a private mediator do not exhibit extreme behavior. They may have a high level of conflict that must be contained or managed by the mediator while it is being resolved, however. Each mediator must determine how complex a situation must be before he or she refuses to handle it in mediation.

REFERENCES

Bethel, C.A., & Singer, L.R. (1982). Mediation: A new remedy for cases of domestic violence. In H. Davidson, L. Ray, & R. Horowitz (Eds.), *Alternative means of family dispute resolution*. Washington, DC: American Bar Association.

Bohannon, P. (1971). The six stations of divorce. In P. Bohannon (Ed.), *Divorce and after*, 33–62. New York: Anchor Books.

Brown, D.G. (1982). Divorce and family mediation: History, review, future directions. *Conciliation Courts Review, 20*(2), 1–44.

Brown, E.M. (1976a). Divorce counseling. In D.H. Olson (Ed.), *Treating relationships*, 399–429. Lake Mills, IA: Graphic Publishing Company.

Brown, E.M. (1976b). A model of the divorce process. *Conciliation Courts Review, 14*(2), 1–11.

Coogler, O.J. (1978). *Structured mediation in divorce settlement: A handbook for marital mediators*. Lexington, MA: D.C. Heath.

Froiland, D.J., & Hozman, T.L. (1977). Counseling for constructive divorce. *Personnel and Guidance Journal, 55*, 525–529.

Goldstein, J., Freud, A., & Solnit, A.J. (1973). *Beyond the best interests of the child*. New York: The Free Press.

Hollingsworth, M. (1984, May). *Mediation bane or boon*. Speech given before the Maryland State Commission for Women, Annapolis.

Ibrahim, A.I. (1984). The process of divorce. *Conciliation Courts Review, 22*(1), 81–95.

Kaslow, F.W. (1981). Divorce and divorce therapy. In A.S. Gurman & D.P. Kniskern (Eds), *Handbook of family therapy*. New York: Brunner/Mazel.

Kessler, S. (1975). *The American way of divorce: Prescriptions for change*. Chicago: Nelson-Hall.

Kressel, K., Jaffee, N., Tuchman, B., Watson, C., & Deutsch, M. (1980). A typology of divorcing couples: Implications for mediation and the divorce process. *Family Process, 19*(2), 101–116.

Kübler-Ross, E. (1969). *On death and dying*. New York: Macmillan.

Wallerstein, J.S., & Kelly, J.B. (1980). *Surviving the breakup: How children and parents cope with divorce*. New York: Basic Books.

Weisman, R.S. (1975). Crisis theory and the process of divorce. *Social Casework, 56*, 205–212.

4. Models of Mediation

Susan M. Brown

DIVORCE MEDIATION COMES IN A VARIETY OF FORMS. EACH FORM reflects the setting in which the service is being offered, the framework from which the mediator shapes his or her process, and the prior profession of the mediator. There are, for instance, attorney mediators, therapist mediators, and labor negotiator mediators. In addition, the effectiveness of the service—as measured by the mediator's settlement rates—is influenced by the style and experience of the mediator; the characteristics and intensity of the conflict being mediated; the verbal skills and IQ of the couple entering the process; the timing of the mediation in the divorce cycle; and, according to some researchers, even the sex and marital status of the mediators (Pearson, Thoennes, & Vanderkooi, 1982; Waldron, Roth, Fair, Mann, & McDermott, 1984).

Despite these variables, each form of divorce mediation is a goal-oriented, problem-solving, helping intervention. The mediator's role is to help participants explore alternate solutions to their conflicts, address the needs of all concerned parties, and develop their own end product, usually a written agreement on all or most of the issues under negotiation. Divorce mediation fosters self-determination, cooperation, and compromise. Usually, clients focus on some or all of the following substantive areas: custody, visitation, division of property, child support, and spousal maintenance (alimony) (Vanderkooi & Pearson, 1983).

The mediator's overall framework or model shapes the type of techniques and subgoals the divorce mediator uses. Three models provide the major frameworks for most mediators: the therapeutic model, the labor negotiations model, and the structured mediation approach of Coogler (1978). Comediation, sometimes treated in the literature as a separate model (Milne, 1983), can be considered a distinctive adaptation of the more basic therapeutic model. While each of these models is fairly easy to distinguish in theory, they are not so cleanly separable in practice. Mediators tend to adopt aspects from each of the models in line with their own training and value orientation, and the characteristics of the couple and conflict being mediated.

THERAPEUTIC MODEL OF MEDIATION

Most forms of divorce mediation have their roots in the therapeutic tradition. At the very least, mediators who are helping a couple decide child-related issues should be knowledgeable in family systems theories, child psychology, and recent theories of child development. Some mediators go even further, claiming that the mediation process itself is a form of agreement-oriented counseling (Irving, 1980) or, more to the point, a kind of strategic therapy (Saposnek, 1984). Thus, Irving (1980) noted:

> Essentially divorce mediation constitutes agreement oriented counseling by a neutral third party directed at persons whose marriage is near breakdown or has already broken down (i.e., divorced). . . . It is a therapeutic process through which the counselor provides an atmosphere in which the marital pair are free to bring out and examine openly their pain. (pp. 46 and 23)

Saposnek (1984) took this view a little further. He believed that it is not sufficient to examine the pain openly; rather,

> like brief strategic therapy, mediation must be viewed as an approach structuring behavioral change . . . it becomes the first step in an ongoing process of building a cooperative co-parenting relationship so that children benefit from positive conflict free relationships with both parents. (p. 46)

Still others have simply pointed out that, while mediation is not therapy, it nearly always has therapeutic effects (Milne, 1978; Ricci, 1980). These range from reducing spousal conflict to increasing individual self-determination and self-worth (Haynes, 1981) and reducing the pain associated with divorce (Coogler, 1978; Irving, 1980).

There are two hallmarks to the therapeutic framework or model. The first is the mediator's insistence that the couple resolve emotional issues before they deal with the substantive issues of the divorce. These emotional aspects are seen as the roots of most substantive conflicts, particularly those involving the children. Milne, a therapeutically oriented divorce mediator, developed a kind of mediation she called family self-determination. Before they negotiate the postdivorce parenting arrangements for their children, her clients are required to produce a marital history as part of their preparation for the emotional divorce. Like Ricci, who also combines mediation with parent training and counseling (Coulson, 1983), Milne views the role of the mediator not just as a facilitator of a settlement, but as an educator. The mediator is charged with the task of educating the couple about the developmental needs of their children, including the need for good parental arrangements post divorce.

This focus on the children and their needs is the second hallmark of the therapeutic model. Coulson (1983), for instance, stated that the mediator's role is to interpret the children's interests realistically to the parents. Irving (1980) made the child's welfare the central responsibility of the mediator, even though he noted that the sessions themselves should be focused on the "family's" needs, not on those of any one family member. Thus, he wrote, "The mediator has an independent goal apart from the narrowly defined interests of the spouses, in that his or her over-riding responsibility is to insure the welfare of the children" (p. 78). He added, "The welfare of the children remains the central focus of all discussion and/or agreements, no matter what the specific topic" (p. 78). "The mediator's main objective is the resolution of family disputes in the context of what is best for the children" (p. 82).

Therapy vs. the Therapeutic Model of Divorce Mediation

As might be expected, therapeutically oriented mediators borrow extensively from the therapeutic skills repertoire of the therapist, rather than the analytic skills of the attorney, in order to settle custody issues. These mediators

- actively listen to the spouses
- bring their feelings to the surface
- defuse their anger
- reframe their conflict
- focus on the couple's rage
- turn the couple from considerations of past injustices to plans for the future
- create an atmosphere of trust and cooperation
- diagnose the couple's level of conflict management skills, their stage in the emotional divorce, and their power balance vis a vis each other (Haynes, 1981; Kelly, 1983).

While this model of mediation may use such therapeutic skills, the service offered is not therapy in the traditional psychotherapeutic sense. Irving (1980) noted that "what makes divorce mediation different from other forms of therapy is that it focuses on relationships between members, rather than concentrating on one particular person" (p. 25). The goal of divorce mediation is not to explore ever deeper levels of psychic tensions, but to develop cooperative co-parenting relationships.

Unlike therapists, however, divorce mediators must have an additional body of knowledge—the legal dimensions of the conflicts being resolved. They must know the relevant local regulations governing the distribution of property, child custody and support, and the seeking and obtaining of a legal divorce. Equally important, the client pool of a divorce mediator is different from that of a therapist. Divorce mediators work with spouses who have *already* decided to divorce, not with couples who are working through this decision. Mediators help these couples to structure this loss as painlessly as possible and to create a contract that can be used to govern both the legal severance of their marital bonds and the continuation of their parental ties.

Furthermore, the client's psychosocial profile, style, and pace do not guide the process, as they frequently do in some forms of therapy (Kelly, 1983). The process of divorce mediation is governed by a structure that has a specific goal: a written agreement. The structure governing the process can be both implicit and explicit, depending on the mediation and the task. For instance, a divorce mediator trained in therapeutic skills can prohibit one party from interrupting another (explicit) and/or reframe the issue in a noninflammatory fashion (implicit). The mediator can manipulate the time between sessions so as to regulate the conflict, allowing time for solutions to be considered or for tensions to decrease, or the mediator can break impasses by offering suggestions for compromise or even leverage with the children, perhaps including them in a session to show the couple the emotional impact of the impasse on the children (Saposnek, 1984). While such tactics may develop from a strategic or crisis therapy model, they are used in mediation to help clients sever an institutionalized relationship and create the forms of a new one, and in addition to modify behavior and improve an ongoing parental relationship.

Finally, not all therapeutic techniques are helpful to divorce mediators. For instance, Vanderkooi and Pearson (1983) found in their research that certain open-ended questions, such as ''Do you have any thoughts on how to begin?'' do not work well in mediation, although they are often used successfully in therapy.

Co-mediation

Therapeutically oriented mediators often establish co-mediation services. A co-mediation team is usually composed of one attorney and one mental health professional, often one woman and one man, sometimes both divorced. This team approach was developed in large measure because therapists wanted to avoid (1) the imposition of their own bias on clients, (2) the unauthorized practice of law, and (3) the dangers of triangling and transference. Co-mediation is thought to meet these concerns in several ways. For example, a co-mediator from a different orientation provides a check against each mediator's bias. In addition, the symmetry of four people reduces the opportunity for clients to triangle the mediator into their conflict.

Co-mediation has several therapeutic and educational benefits not available through sole practitioner mediation services. It provides clients with an example of cooperation both between the sexes and between professionals from different disciplines. If the professionals happen to be divorced, it also provides the clients with a positive model of growth to imitate and allows the co-mediators to conceptualize and identify the clients' concerns vis a vis their status as ex-spouses, but co-parents. There is also an opportunity for creative cross-pollination of ideas and strategies.

The co-mediation model partially answers the criticism that sole mental health practitioners are engaging in the unauthorized practice of law. Gold (1981) and others have noted that, when the attorney acts as traffic manager, defining the issues and providing the technical legal and financial information, and the therapist helps the parents reach an agreement through the use of communication and conflict resource skills, the charge of an unauthorized practice of law may be refuted.

View of the Family Underlying the Therapeutic Approach

Therapeutically oriented mediators tend to see the family as a network of interacting members; this network by nature keeps itself in balance. As Irving (1980) pointed out, "any unusual action by one invariably results in compensating reaction by another" (p. 28). This notion reflects the more basic view that there is a fundamental harmony in the world. Within this view, conflict is not considered to be evil or sick, but rather part of the fabric of family and social life. Conflict is sometimes viewed as constructive if "waged" properly (Trombetta, 1982).

When conflict threatens to disrupt the natural balance within these units, social leaders or authority figures must find ways to return the "natural" balance—to return rationality to the system. Thus, while Irving (1980) noted that divorce is a symptom of the deep-seated distress in our society, he saw the role of the mediator as one of helping spouses "contain" the damage caused by divorce in order to provide children with an atmosphere as conflict free as possible and to restore for them the natural harmony of the family. Deutsch, on the other hand, pointed out that Gresham's Law of Conflict would take over without such mediation of disputes; that is, "the harmful and dangerous elements [would] drive out those which would keep the conflict within bounds" (cited in Irving, 1980, p. 181).

Such a view is compatible with and may even find its roots in the Japanese and Confucian traditions of mediation in which the art of persuasion and compromise is used to settle community and business disputes in a manner compatible with community norms or standards. Compassion is emphasized over justice and moral retaliation. It can also be found in the tradition of Jewish conciliation Boards of Justice—all precursors to divorce mediation as it is practiced today (Folberg, 1983).

Some anthropologists have noted that, if divorce mediators (particularly those operating from a therapeutic framework) are to be effective, it may be necessary for them to practice mediation within a society in which values are shared, the mediator is an authority figure with a background similar to that of the disputants, and the disputants will be involved in an ongoing relationship, as in a business or labor situation, that makes a mediated settlement imperative (Trombetta, 1982). Divorce mediators who provide court-connected services or who work from neighborhood justice centers or other public agencies may come closer to duplicating these conditions than do those who provide services in the private sector. (There are now at least 53 such public divorce mediation services, according to Pearson, Ring, and Milne's 1983 survey.)

Thirteen states now offer or require court-connected mediation of child custody and visitation disputes (Pearson, Thoennes, & Vanderkooi, 1982). These mediations are conducted by the court's staff psychologists or social workers, who also do child custody evaluations for the court. The judge (authority) orders the family to try mediation; if the mediation fails, the mediator may become a source of information for the judge. Although there is clearly no necessarily shared background between client, mediator, and judge in court-connected mediation, the standard for determining the resolution of the dispute is likely to be in line with the community standard of the client (i.e., the best interest of the child standard), at least as reflected in the law. Mediation provided through neighborhood justice centers is performed by volunteers from the community (shared background), and there is an element of coercion (police references) to push the clients into an arena where the resolution of their disputes will allow both to maintain their community membership.

While it may appear that mediation in both these arenas is tainted by elements of coercion, recent research reveals otherwise. Indeed, Sanders

(1983) pointed out that this slight coercive element is exactly what is needed to get some clients—particularly those with intense conflicts—to commit themselves to mediation. Once the commitment has been made, the process promotes self-determination as effectively as if it had been sought voluntarily.

Given this view of the family as a harmonious self-regulating system, divorce mediators who put the children's interests first must realize that they can meet the children's needs only if the parents are also meeting their own needs. In this manner, conflict is avoided, harmony restored, the mediator's neutrality maintained, and the autonomy of each member of the family preserved. The problem, of course, is in the assumptions that these interests are always compatible and that there is in fact a natural harmony to the family—indeed, to the structure of society. It is not always possible, unfortunately, to contain conflict in ways that allow *all* family members' needs to be met without any winners or losers. It may be better to make the welfare of the children paramount not because of this potential ideal of harmony, but because (1) the unfinished business of the marriage partnership is the children and, when dissolving any partnership, paramount consideration should be given to unfinished business; (2) children are the most vulnerable members of the family; (3) the laws within which divorce mediation takes place hold that the children's interest is paramount; (4) most parents are unselfish enough to put their children's welfare before their own interests; and (5) in many areas, the interests of the children can be shown to merge with those of the parents.

LABOR NEGOTIATIONS MODEL OF MEDIATION

The most visible and familiar model of mediation is that found in the labor-management relations field and in the settlement of international and civil rights disputes (Bahr, 1981). While the therapeutic model of divorce mediation predominates in court-connected services, which deal with child custody and visitation issues, the labor-based model is influential in divorce mediation in the private sector.

Similarities between Labor Mediation and Divorce Mediation

Many features of labor mediation are also characteristic of divorce mediation, regardless of its orientation. First, according to Markowitz and Enfram (1984), the mediator acts not as an authority figure, but serves as a facilitator and catalyst in both labor and divorce mediation. The mediator offers assistance, but does not judge the merits of either party's position. The mediator does not focus on personalities, but emphasizes positions, interpersonal relationships, and services. Second, mediators in both arenas work to help the parties reach a written settlement. Third, neither labor mediation nor divorce mediation allows a laissez faire attitude to dominate the negotiations. Fourth, unlike commercial transactions, which need never reach closure, labor-management negotiations and divorce mediation must always result in settlement, or the conflict will be resolved for the disputants by others in a different forum. Fifth, both labor and family disputes are polycentric or many-sided and, according to Folberg (1983), relationships in both arenas are "long term and depend on further cooperation of the parties in contrast to isolated disputes that depend for their resolution on findings of historical fact for the purpose of deciding on a winner and a loser who need have no further dealings" (p. 5).

Divorce mediators who use the labor framework borrow various techniques from labor mediation. For instance, to ensure that the high emotional level associated with divorce settlement discussions does not sabotage or obstruct the settlement process, the mediator employs the labor negotiation techniques of individual caucuses and shuttle diplomacy. These help the divorce mediator learn each party's real interests and emotional attachments. The separate meetings also help the mediator to gain the trust and cooperation of each spouse, as well as to identify areas of agreement in order to reduce the number of issues that must be resolved through bargaining. In an effort to encourage better bargaining, other labor negotiation techniques, such as reducing disputant expectations and stressing the consequences of failure to come to agreement, are also employed. Both the labor mediator and the divorce mediator working from the labor negotiations framework use the tool of nonreversible concessions to ensure that the process does not backslide.

Perhaps most important, unlike divorce mediators who use other frameworks and close off one area or issue before solving the next group of issues, divorce mediators who use a labor negotiations model are likely to reserve closure on major disputes until agreement on the entire package has been reached. Toward this end, they trade off items between and within issue areas in order to obtain a final package (Haynes, 1981).

Labor and divorce mediators have other elements in common that tend to disassociate them from divorce mediators who use different approaches. For instance, if labor-based divorce mediators were to describe their role as that of an advocate, it would be as an advocate of the process of negotiating itself, rather than as an advocate of the children or the family's welfare.

One of the hallmarks of the labor-based model is its reliance on the process of negotiation itself to produce a fair settlement. This is done through successive bargaining, rather than through extensive education of the couple about their parenting responsibilities or through adherence to a set of rules. Indeed, in this model, the mediator may even encourage the children to take greater charge of the direction of their future lives.

This process of increasing the self direction of family members takes place gradually. First, in selecting mediation, the partners have already opted for cooperation, rather than litigation or competition (Haynes, 1981). Second, labor-oriented divorce mediators have their clients talk about their relationship—bring the anger to the surface—before beginning to negotiate the severance or change in their relationship. If the couple is not able to move beyond the anger to negotiate substantive issues, the mediator either refers the couple out for therapy or clearly stops the mediation and assumes the role of therapist to help the clients deal with the emotions blocking the negotiations. Third, it is assumed that the negotiations will take place within a value structure that is determined by the parties' own sense of fairness, rather than by the mediator's sense of fairness or the rules. If the mediator sees that the couple has lost sight of the interests of other family members, such as the children, the mediator represents those interests to the parents in order to keep the negotiations on track. The mediator's allegiance is to the process, not to the individual partners or to their children.

The labor-based divorce mediator tends to assume that the negotiation process is at base monetarily oriented, regardless of the substantive issues being discussed, and helps each side bargain for the best possible financial settlement. This is often done either through the use of integrative solutions in which joint utility is maximized or through the use of distributive solutions, compromises, or trade-offs in which clients are persuaded to accept the solutions on the grounds of fairness and reasonableness (Vanderkooi & Pearson, 1983). In either case, clients are free to employ attorneys to review their settlements as they are being made and/or to help them negotiate more forcefully. Such a practice is usually, although not always, avoided in the therapeutic model, because references to attorneys are thought to jeopardize the cooperative atmosphere being nurtured by the mediator.

Differences between Labor Mediation and Divorce Mediation

In labor mediations, the final contract calls for basically minor contingent changes in what is essentially an ongoing, permanent relationship between two institutions (Markowitz & Enfram, 1984). In divorce mediation, the final contract governs the severance of what was once an institutionalized relationship—that of a married couple—and creates the boundaries, roles, and structure for a new institutionalized relationship—that of divorced parents. The private aspects of parenting ties, once the unwritten product of custom and habit, are now regulated by a written structure that has the force of law. Furthermore, these parental ties, unlike the more permanent labor-management ties, will weaken and disappear as the children reach adulthood.

Since it is assumed that it will not be necessary to renegotiate divorce settlements, particularly those arrived at in mediation, it is essential that settlements be fair. Labor contracts, on the other hand, are subject to cyclical, frequent bargaining sessions. Hence, their "fairness" is not so crucial. Thus, the equalizing of the power balance between spouses is more important in divorce mediation than in labor mediation. It is for this reason that Haynes (1981) and others emphasize empowerment of individual family members. The mediator must help spouses understand and accept the fact that they have the right to "fight" for their own interests, even when they differ from those of other family members.

The interpersonal dynamics are more complex in labor mediation than in divorce mediation (Markowitz & Enfram, 1984). The divorce mediator generally deals with neophyte bargainers who are without constituencies and are often at a time of low self-esteem (Haynes, 1981). In labor negotiations, however, the mediator and the negotiators can play to constituencies for leverage (Markowitz & Enfram, 1984). Since the bargainers are experienced negotiators, the mediator is free to rely on manipulative techniques unavailable in the divorce setting.

When an impasse, such as a strike, occurs during labor mediation, the mediation can continue in its shadow. When there is an impasse in divorce mediation, however, the mediation must stop until the impasse has been resolved.

STRUCTURED MEDIATION

Introduced in 1974 by Coogler, an attorney with family systems and transactional analysis training, structured mediation shares many of the characteristics of the other models. It, too, is intended to eliminate unnecessary suffering in divorce, to promote cooperative problem solving on the part of the disputants, and to open lines of communication between parents and their children. Like the labor-based model, it focuses on maintaining negotiations between spouses at a balanced and goal-oriented level. Unlike other models, however, structured mediation relies heavily on a set of rules, a procedural structure to guide rationality, to foster cooperation, and to reduce pain.

These rules are derived from at least two sources: (1) the Uniform Marriage and Divorce Act and (2) state laws in those states that had substantially revised their divorce laws before 1978 (Grebe, in press). These rules are supported by the Family Mediation Association. Before they enter the mediation process, clients sign a contract agreeing to adhere to these rules and enforce them.

Coogler borrowed a great deal from Morton Deutsch, who argued in his book *The Resolution of Conflict* (1973) that conflict could be limited and controlled by institutional forums, social roles, rules for negotiations, and specific procedures (Grebe, in press). In adjudication and litigation, the institutional rules require that negotiations be adversarial and that outcomes produce a winner and a loser. In mediation, however, the institutional rules require that negotiations be cooperative, produce open communication, establish an atmosphere of trust, and encourage self-determination. Unlike therapeutically oriented models and labor negotiations models, which center the family's balance in its inherent structure, Coogler's model creates a rule-governed structure that imparts to the family and to the process the balance necessary to create a fair settlement, one in which there are no victims.

While it is essential to understand interpersonal dynamics, Coogler believed that the key to fair agreement was adherence to the structure or rules he devised. These detailed procedures and definitions encourage spouses to fight for what they need, but to do so fairly and rationally. The structure itself

- ensures confidentiality by prohibiting the use of information disclosed in the sessions in litigation
- requires full disclosure of assets and personal information
- provides mechanisms to ensure that disputants commit themselves to the mediation and maintain that commitment throughout
- enables the disputants to gain a balance of power *prior* to beginning mediation
- assures disputants of the neutrality of the mediator
- assures the mediator that his or her own values will not be compromised by an unfair settlement

- requires the orderly, timely progression of dispute resolution to ensure that mediation does not become sidetracked or mired in the "emotional" underpinnings of divorce

Commitment in Structured Mediation

The structure contains several rules that help produce and maintain commitment to the process. First, the disputants must deposit an amount sufficient to cover 10 mediation sessions (Coogler, 1978). Second, they must agree that, if they are unable to resolve an issue after a certain length of time spent negotiating, they will submit that issue to arbitration. Third, before they begin the process, they sign a contract in which they confirm their understanding of the rules, roles, and definitions and agree to proceed by them. Sometimes, an interim agreement, to be in effect just for the duration of the mediation, is also reached in the first session. Such an agreement shows the couple that they can cooperate (Coogler, 1978). This way of achieving commitment to the process differs from the court-connected therapeutically oriented mediator's reliance on an element of coercion and from the labor-based mediator's search for "signs" of such commitment, such as the source of the referral, the completion of assigned tasks, and the stage of the emotional divorce in which the clients find themselves.

Equalization of Power

The rules equalize the power of the spouses before, instead of during, the process of bargaining. Since they explicitly delineate roles for each party and for the mediator that require cooperative problem solving, the rules help to eliminate bargaining from positions of immovable power. They not only specifically define such substantive issues as child support, custody, and marital property, but also set out guidelines for division of property and for child placement that are consistent with state laws and fundamental rules of equity, making it easier for couples who are naive bargainers to bargain effectively and fairly. By requiring that the couple read, understand, and agree to these rules before mediation can begin, each spouse starts with the same criteria for decision making.

The shuttle diplomacy and individual caucusing used by labor-oriented divorce mediators are prohibited in structured mediation. It is believed that these tactics may prove detrimental by appearing to alter the mediator's neutrality or by, in fact, destroying the atmosphere of trust created by the rules. As Grebe (in press) noted in her article describing structured mediation:

> Since the issue of trust is fundamental to the success of mediation (Deutsch, 1973), Coogler maintained that individual meetings or phone calls were more counterproductive than helpful. This absence of an opportunity to sway the mediator protects the integrity of the mediation process and the role of the mediator. (p. 8)

The issues of trust, cooperation, and impartiality of the mediator underlie several other important rules. For example, at the end of the mediation, the rules require the couple to submit their memorandum of understanding to an advisory attorney who will review it to determine its legal implications. If the attorney's suggestions for change require further negotiations, the attorney withdraws from the consultation, and the couple returns to mediation. The rules prohibit the use of a separate attorney for each spouse either to assist during the negotiations or to review the agreement before it is signed. Both options are available under other models.

Resolution of Issues

In the labor model and in some therapeutic models, mediators are free to work on all issues simultaneously, winnowing out areas of agreement so as to reduce the number of issues that must be resolved. Once this has been done, the bargaining can begin. Often, this bargaining goes on across issue areas, as well as within them. Furthermore, most labor-based models, taking their cue from successful labor negotiations, encourage mediators to hold up final agreements on various issue areas until agreement has been reached in all areas. In this way, last minute trading between two stubborn points—often in different issue areas—can be used to cement the agreement.

Coogler, in contrast, requires disputants to proceed from issue to issue in a set order: custody, then property, then support (child and spousal). The order is set because, according to Coogler, the issues of custody and property must be resolved before an adequate and fair amount of either child or spousal support can be determined. Within each issue area, however, acceptable points of agreement can be removed from negotiations. The difference between this model and others is that, once an issue has been resolved, it is closed; it is not reopened unless the mediator, not the couple, deems it necessary. Like labor-based mediators, Coogler believed that most custody fights are primarily squabbles over money. Thus, if the couple prove intractable on custody, an exception may be made and custody tabled until after the support issue has been determined.

Coogler's model shares the therapeutic concept of the naturalness of conflict, but deals with this assumption differently. While labor-based and therapeutic mediators use an elastic time frame in which conflict can be diffused and resolved, Coogler believed that emotion and conflicts tended to intensify and defeat rationality over time. Thus, he required clients to adhere to a prescribed schedule of sessions, spaced a week apart, and optimally expected a settlement after six to eight sessions.

Finally, while all mediation models acknowledge the importance and presence of a value dimension, there is a difference in the way they make this dimension explicit. In structured mediation, the rules governing the mediation contain explicit values that are based on fundamental principles of fairness and the prevailing legal standards. In agreeing to follow this structure, the participants have agreed to work within the same value framework. Yet, even within this framework, the couple may reach an agreement that the mediator feels is unjust. The rules allow the mediator to disavow the agreement.

By contrast, labor-based models tend to assume that people will be fair with each other once the emotional underpinning and anger are brought to the surface, acknowledged, and contained (Haynes, 1981)—a process dependent in some measure on the skills of the mediator. In therapeutically oriented mediation, fair settlements are encouraged and made possible by focusing the couple on what is best for the children.

CONCLUSION

While these three models emphasize different techniques and pose different tasks for their clients, they overlap in many of their subsidiary goals. In both structured mediation and its labor-based counterpart, for instance, the need to balance the power of the disputants is stressed, and the issue of economic independence is considered the crucial task of mediators. Finally, like therapeutically oriented divorce mediators, those who use structured mediation believe that their process has an educational component and that their clients will be able to use their approach to resolve future conflict. Haynes (1981) clearly advocated negotiation as a process of self-development for greater autonomy in future decision making.

The value in knowing these different approaches then may be in helping clients seeking a divorce mediator to eliminate certain orientations that require tasks *not* relevant to their dispute.

To make an informed choice, potential mediation clients must interview mediators to determine each mediator's general orientation, level of experience, flexibility in accommodating the process to the couple's own perceived needs, negotiating style, and value structure.

If, for instance, child custody is not an issue and the disputants are not enmeshed emotionally, but need only what attorney Larry Gaughan has called "capstone" mediation (Blades, 1984, p. 92), it seems unnecessary for them to enter a mediation in which they must supply a lengthy marital history or a mediation that calls for shuttle diplomacy. On the other hand, if the couple has not yet worked through their anger or if they are at different stages of the divorce process, but need an agreement that will shield their children from their conflict, then a therapeutically oriented mediator might be most helpful. If the couple has a great many conflicts and a rather limited time frame, however, the structured approach may be more effective.

In any event, recent research on labor mediation has indicated that, regardless of the framework and the issues involved, the style of the mediator is important. It appears that aggressive/directive mediators are more successful than less directive ones in helping couples move through the issues, although they are not necessarily more effective in producing final settlements. Pearson's studies showed that the most effective mediators—in terms of reaching settlement—were those using an approach with a great deal of mediator input (Vanderkooi & Pearson, 1983). Waldron and associates (1984), in a review of 13 court-connected mediations, found that mixed sex co-mediators were the most successful, with the least successful being co-mediator teams in which both are women. Pearson and others have confirmed that, whatever the variables and their significance, the most important ingredient for success—in terms of settlement rates—is the experience of the mediator (Vanderkooi & Pearson, 1983).

REFERENCES

Bahr, S.J. (1981). An evaluation of court mediation. *Journal of Family Issues, 2*(1), 39–60.

Blades, J. (1984). Mediation: An old art revitalized. *Mediation Quarterly 3,* 59–98.

Coogler, O.J. (1978). *Structural mediation in divorce settlement.* Lexington, MA: D.C. Heath.

Coogler, O.J., Weber, R., & McHenry, P. (1979). Divorce mediation: A means of facilitating divorce adjustment. *The Family Coordinator, 28*(2), 255–263.

Coulson, R. (1983). *Fighting fair*. New York: The Free Press.

Deutsch, M. (1973). *The resolution of conflict*. New Haven: Yale University Press.

Folberg, J. (1983). A mediation overview: History and dimensions of practice. *Mediation Quarterly, 1*, 3–14.

Gold, L. (1981). The psychological context of the interdisciplinary team model in marital dissolution. Unpublished paper.

Grebe, S. (In press). Structured mediation and its variants: What makes it unique? In J. Folberg & A. Milne (Eds.), *Divorce mediation: Theory and practice*. New York: Guilford Press.

Haynes, J.M. (1981). *Divorce mediation*. New York: Springer.

Irving, H.H. (1980). *Divorce mediation*. New York: Universe Books.

Kelly, J.B. (1983). Mediation and psychotherapy: Distinguishing the differences. *Mediation Quarterly, 1*, 33–45.

Markowitz, J., & Enfram, P. (1984). Mediation in labor disputes and divorces: A comparative analysis. *Mediation Quarterly, 2*, 67–78.

Milne, A. (1978). Family self determination: An alternative to the adversarial system in custody disputes. *Conciliation Courts Review, 16*(2), 1–10.

Milne, A. (1983). Divorce mediation: The state of the art. *Mediation Quarterly, 1*, 15–33.

Pearson, J., Ring, M., & Milne, A. (1983). A portrait of divorce mediation services in the public and private sector. *Conciliation Courts Review, 21*(1), 1–24.

Pearson, J., Thoennes, N., & Vanderkooi, L. (1982). The decision to mediate: Profiles of individuals who accept and reject the opportunity to mediate contested child custody and visitation issues. In E. Fisher & M. Fisher (Eds.), *Therapists, lawyers, and divorcing spouses*. New York: Haworth Press, 65–76.

Ricci, I. (1980). *Mom's house, dad's house*. New York: Macmillan.

Sanders, F. (1983). Family mediation: Problems and prospects. *Mediation Quarterly 2*, 3–12.

Saposnek, D.T. (1984). Strategies in child custody mediation: A family systems approach. *Mediation Quarterly, 2*, 29–54.

Trombetta, D. (1982). Custody evaluation and custody mediation: A comparison of two dispute interventions. In E. Fisher & M. Fisher (Eds.), *Therapists, lawyers, and divorcing spouses*. New York: Haworth Press, 65–76.

Vanderkooi, L., & Pearson, J. (1983). Mediating divorce disputes: Mediator behaviors, styles and roles. *Family Relations*, 557–566.

Waldron, J., Roth, C., Fair, P., Mann, E., & McDermott, Jr., J. (1984). A therapeutic mediation model for child custody dispute resolution. *Mediation Quarterly*, 5–20.

5. Marital Assessment as an Option in Divorce Mediation

Lori Heyman Gordon

IF MARRIAGE AND FAMILY THERAPISTS WERE TRAINED AS DIVORCE mediators, they could use their skills as marital therapists to help couples make more informed decisions regarding separation and divorce. A marital assessment can lead the couple seeking divorce mediation to a less punitive attitude toward divorce or to a more hopeful view of the possibility of repairing the marriage. Marriage and family therapists who have received training as divorce mediators are in an ideal position to offer this marital assessment option to couples who seek their help for divorce mediation.

The husbands and wives who appear at my office requesting divorce mediation arrive with separate and often intensely emotional agendas. One spouse generally believes that he or she is clearly seeking to end the marriage and hopes to end it in a nonadversarial, cooperative manner. The other is often in a frozen state of reluctance, secretly hoping that some way can be found to illuminate and repair the marital difficulties.

Mr. S., aged 32, was a dark-haired government scientist of medium build. He was dressed in a dark business suit. His jaw was set. He had come for help with a mediated separation and divorce. He voiced no doubt that his love for his wife had died. He had tried over the previous year, but had been unable to change his feelings of resentment and anger in the relationship. After a lengthy period of despair, he had decided that there was no hope for his marriage and he had to leave.

Mrs. S., a neatly dressed, slightly plump young woman of 31, sat quietly, looking somewhat sad. When she spoke, she expressed confusion about the reasons for her husband's anger and decision to leave. They had two small children, born a year apart. Recently, her husband had become more aloof and distant from the children. She did not understand what was happening in their relationship, why he was angry, or why he wanted to leave. She wanted the marriage.

Deciding to explore further, I said that many things that go wrong in relationships are the result of enormous misunderstandings, misperceptions, or erroneous assumptions. I added that this is no one's fault; people simply do not always have the tools or the objectivity to understand what has gone wrong. I asked if Mr. S. would be willing to meet with me once individually to help me understand what had happened to so disillusion him with his marital relationship. I also asked to meet once with Mrs. S. Then, I requested a meeting with the two of them together to tell them of my observations. I pointed out that, even if it was too late for their marriage, it was important that they both understand what had happened so that they did not repeat the same patterns in the future. In addition, as they had two children, they must be able to cooperate in the future in behalf of their children. Both agreed to come.

In my session with Mr. S., I discovered that he was the only child of a mother who had been bedridden with a chronic illness throughout most of his childhood. He felt that his mother's illness had deprived him of her attention and nurturance through his formative years, and he had much residual anger at his mother. He had met his wife in graduate school. They spent all their time together, studied together, and went to class together; he found her constant friendship and companionship a healing factor in his life. He fell in love. They continued to pursue joint careers and to make all decisions jointly. Their decision to have children was joint.

Things began to go wrong after the birth of their first child. Suddenly, his wife was always tired, made decisions without consulting him, and did not seek him out to find out what was bothering him when he withdrew. Then, their second son was born. While he loved the children, he felt less and less for his wife. By then, she was not only tired, but also frazzled; made many decisions about the house, the furnishings, and the children without consulting him; and did not seem even to notice when he withdrew. He felt more and more unloved. Finally, his career took a downward turn. His wife, who had been his confidant, was too busy or tired to seem interested or available. He decided the marriage was not meeting his needs. There was no reason to stay. He rented an apartment.

In my session with Mrs. S., I found that she was one of four children in a family in which everyone cooperated to get the work done. There was no question that the task came first. Hers had been a calm family, with no explosions and little need for confidences. Her parents' marriage had been devoted and longlasting. She never questioned the bonds of the love or loyalty in her family. Later, in her own marriage, she took it for granted that her husband would understand her fatigue and the need to put the care of their two very young children first. She did not know why he held these things against her. She assumed it was an immature attitude that he would outgrow. She was shocked and dismayed when he demanded a divorce. She felt confused and discouraged; she wanted help with the marriage.

The joint session was a combination of teaching and theorizing. I reviewed their individual histories, the ties that drew them together, and the experiences they had shared. I then pointed out the dissimilarities in their histories, the expectations of each that had not been verbalized, and the disappointments that stemmed from these unverbalized and, thus, often hidden expectations. I pointed out the disappointment and unhappiness that his mother's illness and unavailability had caused Mr. S. I theorized that the strain on his wife caused by the care of the two children left him feeling that she had withdrawn from him, as his mother had, and that he had transferred his anger at his mother to his wife, even though the circumstances were vastly different. I noted the different history of Mrs. S. and her unquestioning assumption that he would understand her need to nurture the children and to make decisions on the spot, respecting her intelligence and autonomy without questioning her love or loyalty. Both husband and wife listened intently, nodding as they recognized their own expectations and assumptions. I then suggested that change might come about through participation in an intensive weekend workshop on understanding self and relationships. Both Mr. and Mrs. S. agreed to attend.

At the workshop, Mr. S. had an opportunity to do some individual work on his anger and disappointment. As his anger emerged, he was better able to reflect on his understanding—or lack of it—with his wife in their current situation. He gradually became less angry and more aware that he had been blaming her for many things she could not control and had been expecting her to understand his feelings and needs without being told about them. By the end of the weekend, he was open to a new decision about his marriage. He and his wife chose to attend a 4-month seminar on relationships. He cancelled his lease on his separate apartment and joined an individual ongoing therapy group to work on his own issues for the next several months. At last contact, Mr. and Mrs. S. were proceeding happily as a family.

As a marriage and family therapist of some 20 years, I have developed a variety of formats to help couples repair dysfunctional marriages. If they still choose to part, the goal is to help them part with less bitterness and less destructiveness than is typical in our adversarial system of divorce. By using the technique of divorce mediation developed by Coogler (1978), I hoped to help a couple part cooperatively, able to collaborate in the future on behalf of their children and in any other involvements that must continue.

My expectations received a severe jolt when I asked my first couple requesting mediation what each one hoped would come out of our session together. The discrepancy between their separate hopes, experiences, and agendas, as well as the discrepancies between those of succeeding couples, revealed that it was not enough to resolve the practical mediation issues. First, the couple needed to acquire a deeper understanding of the causes of the deterioration of their marriage. They needed to determine whether there were factors as yet unknown to them that might help them to repair their relationship or at least to part with less bitterness, less destructiveness, and more awareness of what each had contributed to the marital dissolution. Before proceeding with mediation with a couple, I decided to offer an option for an assessment of their marriage. This option would include my observations regarding the factors that had contributed to their marital dysfunction. Of the first 10 couples who presented themselves for mediation, 6 accepted the assessment option.

The format includes an initial joint interview with the couple to explore the history of their marriage, as well as the disappointments, resentments, and behaviors that have harmed their relationship. This is a 1½- to 2-hour session, with the emphasis clearly on gathering data. I then hold a 1½- to 2-hour individual session with each partner. In this session, we discuss family history; models from the parental marriage; sibling relationships; early decisions and experiences regarding love, trust, caring, competition, and power; communication styles; and marital role expectations. I pointedly track every belief, expectation, or life decision made that has affected the marital relationship, including invisible loyalties (Boszormenyi-Nagy & Spark, 1973), changes in the life cycle and in the relationship cycle, the impact of children, job changes, communication impasses, the way in which disappointments were handled, and lost hopes and dreams. The individual session generally establishes an attitude of openness and growing curiosity in the client as to the unique and specific history and conditioning that each has brought to the relationship and the way in which particular styles and expectations have meshed or failed to mesh with those of the partner. Each of these individual sessions leads to new understandings. Often an additional individual session is needed to explore further data.

After the individual sessions with each member of the couple, I again meet jointly with the two of them for a feedback session. I review the data collected and offer my view of what has led to their marital difficulties. I relabel and reframe many of their behaviors and intentions, pointing out that the issue was seldom blame, but was rather the lack of information as a result of enormous misunderstanding or misperception. I offer possible formats for change, such as individual, couple, or group therapy; intensive weekend behavior modification workshops; or a 4-month seminar (PAIRS) developed for the specific purpose of practicing and improving intimate relationship skills.

Of the six couples who accepted the marital assessment option, three chose to work on their marriages and stayed together. They worked in individual and couple therapy for 3 to 6 months. Of the three couples who separated, one partner in each was already involved with another lover. Within the next 8 months, one of these ended his extramarital relationship and returned to his marriage. Those who went on with mediation appeared better able to handle the strain and loss of parting because of the opportunity that they had been given to reflect upon and examine their relationship. They seemed better able to accept the ending of their marriage nonpunitively.

A dispassionate assessment of the factors leading to marital breakdown has many benefits. In some instances, the assessment and subsequent treatment recommendations can restore the marriage to a more fulfilling level and enable it to continue. In other instances, it can lead to a far less punitive, less bitter parting, enhancing each partner's acceptance of the other's humanity and each partner's ability to cooperate with the other in resolving future problems. Finally, in deepening the couple's understanding of those factors that have contributed to the breakdown of the marital relationship, the assessment offers a measure of prevention against repetition of those patterns in succeeding relationships.

Those couples who did not choose the option of the assessment were still markedly interested in knowing it was available; those couples who accepted it learned a great deal regarding their attitudes, emotions, and behaviors. Those couples who chose to work on their relationship restored their marriages to a level of functioning and gratification higher than its previous level by developing the understanding and skills, with each other, that had been missing.

In summary, the marital assessment option is offered at a specific point in time, with a limited goal. It is not a treatment, but is the basis for further reflection on a major life decision—a decision that affects many people. It is an opportunity to uncover data that can be of crucial value in decision making. It does not involve an unlimited, ongoing therapy contract, however. It is a time-limited, short-term, goal-oriented, psychoeducational service.

REFERENCES

Boszormenyi-Nagy, I., & Spark, G. (1973). *Invisible loyalties.* New York: Harper & Row.

Coogler, O.J. (1978). *Structured mediation in divorce settlement.* Lexington, MA: Lexington Books.

6. Co-Mediation: Pros and Cons

Martin A. Kranitz

Wʜᴇɴ ᴜsᴇᴅ ᴀᴘᴘʀᴏᴘʀɪᴀᴛᴇʟʏ, ᴄᴏ-ᴍᴇᴅɪᴀᴛɪᴏɴ ᴛᴇᴀᴍs ᴄᴀɴ ʀᴇꜰʟᴇᴄᴛ much of what must take place between separating or divorcing spouses. The disadvantages of co-mediation are real, but not insurmountable, and co-mediators are able to use additional techniques that are not available to single mediators. Furthermore, the opportunity for co-mediators to provide both positive and negative feedback to each other with regard to techniques, knowledge, and skill is invaluable from the standpoint of personal and professional growth.

REVIEW OF THE LITERATURE

There is little agreement in the literature about the practice of co-mediation. For example, there are several views on appropriate composition of the ideal co-mediation team. Some authors believe that the team should have both male and female members; others, that the teams should comprise lawyers and therapists. Finally, some believe that the ideal co-mediation team is made up of a lawyer and a therapist, one of whom is male and the other female (Black & Joffee, 1978; Gold, 1982; Wiseman & Fiske, 1980).

Folberg (1982) stated that interdisciplinary co-mediation teams present "the most flexible approach in relation to a theory of divorce mediation, which stresses the interplay of emotional resolution with the comprehensive legal settlement task" (p. 39). Folberg (1982) also indicated that when a co-mediation team consists of a lawyer and a therapist, the team not only can separate emotional and legal issues, but also can deal with them simultaneously. If, in addition, the co-mediators are male and female, sexual issues and roles can be handled by example as well as by discussion. "Triangling" can also be controlled. The same thought was reflected by Salius (cited in D. Brown, 1982) when he stated that male and female co-mediation teams provide a balanced sexual perspective, equalize relationships, and reduce power struggles between divorcing couples. Male and female teams enable the couple to identify with, or relate to, a person of the same or opposite sex, depending on their particular orientation.

Similarly, Wiseman and Fiske (1980) suggested that a lawyer-therapist team presents "a synthesis of special skills of the social worker and the legal knowledge of the attorney" (p. 443). In their model, the attorney and the social worker provide "a flexible series of consultations with the couple working toward future resolution of marital breakdown" (p. 444). They stressed that separation and divorce are not necessarily the goal of mediation. The couple can be helped to negotiate power imbalances as well as to gain insight into their difficulties so that they can plan solutions or alternate approaches. The lawyer provides a framework within which the couple may begin to talk and listen to each other on various levels. (The lawyer may also draft a separation agreement, when appropriate.) From the information provided by the attorney, the therapist forms some hypotheses about the psychological, psychiatric, and sociological factors that contributed to the marital crisis. The therapist may also suggest ways in which the attorney can deal with resistance or impasse.

Wiseman and Fiske believed that one of the benefits of such a team is that it provides a system of checks and balances among the mediators. The lawyer may be tempted to hurry toward a separation agreement, but the therapist slows the process to give the couple more time for a deeper understanding of their problems. It appears that this model does not require both the co-mediators to be present for all sessions, although they are to collaborate with each other between their separate sessions and discuss appropriate lines of action or interaction. This is a slightly different approach, since co-mediators are generally both present during all sessions.

Black and Joffee (1978) described the role of the attorney more as an arbitrator who provides nonadversarial legal advice and counsel, and guides couples through the negotiation process; they described the therapist as a "facilitator and divorce counselor." Others who support co-mediation include Gaybrick and Bryner (1981), Nichols and Troester (1979), and Wyckoff and Cleveland (1980).

Specific criticisms of co-mediation usually revolve around its cost effectiveness for the couple or the lack of freedom and flexibility for the mediators. With regard to cost effectiveness, it has been noted that co-mediation would probably occur more frequently in a public rather than a private setting. In fact, the states of Connecticut and Minnesota provide for co-mediation. The King County Family Court Mediation Program in Seattle, Washington, has used a panel of three mediators, consisting of a lawyer, a psychologist, and a psychiatrist (Folberg, 1982).

The only research study dealing with co-mediation was conducted at the Denver Custody Mediation Project (Pearson, cited in D. Brown, 1982). No significant difference in outcome was found between mediations conducted by single mediators and those conducted by co-mediator teams made up of interdisciplinary, male-female teams.

PROS

Two mediators generally bring more knowledge, more resources, and more control to the mediation setting than one mediator can bring, especially if the co-mediators are an attorney and a mental health counselor. Not only does each have a special knowledge developed through personal experience and practice in his or her profession, but also each has additional resources on which to draw. Furthermore, co-mediators demonstrate for the couple an interaction of professional activity and knowledge focused on helping them. The couple can see that their emotional, legal, and economic needs are being dealt with by a team that has prior experience and training in these areas. Such a team also provides great flexibility in the ways that issues may be handled.

The issue of control is quite important in mediation, since any individual may try to be controlling, overbearing, or aggressive at any given time. Sadly, this may be true of a mediator as well. It is common for one spouse to attempt to take control throughout a session or series of sessions, in spite of the mediator's attempts to establish a balance. The use of co-mediators, regardless of their professional training, makes it more difficult for one person to become overbearing or overcontrolling. Any attempt at control can be diffused, to a certain extent, by co-mediators who are able to alternate back and forth in terms of their interactions with the couple and with each other to help reestablish a balanced communication system.

There is an obvious benefit to a male-female co-mediation team, since this provides a clear role model/sex model interchange for the couple. In addition, as mentioned earlier, the use of such a team allows each spouse to identify with either the same sex or opposite sex mediator, or to alternate between them as needed. When a male-female team co-mediates, it is less likely that the spouses will "project" behaviors or feelings that they attribute to their spouse to the mediator. Co-mediation by same sex mediators can be done successfully, however, if it is done cautiously and conscientiously. It is necessary for both mediators to check regularly with both spouses to determine whether they are sensing any prejudice or bias. It is necessary to check with both spouses because, if the co-mediators are both male, for example, it is not always the wife who feels overwhelmed and unbalanced; the husband may feel that the male mediators are forming a protective shield around the wife, thus setting up an imbalanced negotiating system. It is therefore necessary for both mediators to reaffirm with both spouses that mediation is taking place in a balanced and equitable fashion.

Even when the co-mediation team is not mixed in terms of professional background, they may bring specialized information into the co-mediation setting. If the co-mediators know that they will be working together on numerous cases, they may wish to specialize in certain subareas of expertise. For example, one mediator may take a particular interest in taxes and estate planning; the other, in pensions, health insurance, and co-parenting issues. Although all mediators would ideally have experience, knowledge, and sensitivity in all areas of mediation, it is obviously not practical to expect mediators to attend all training programs to upgrade their skills. Rather, co-mediators may divide this educational process.

Co-mediation provides mediators with a system of checks and balances. In spite of a mediator's best efforts and numerous checklists, it is always possible to overlook an item, an issue, or a detail. Even the experienced mediator may be overwhelmed by the avalanche of information that the couple is providing. There are times when something said by one spouse may go unnoticed by a single mediator, but be noticed by the co-mediator. This is also true of nonverbal cues, such as body language. When this happens, the co-mediator can intercede, pointing out significant comments or actions and proceed either in the same direction or on a parallel course so that little, if any, ground is lost.

Co-mediators are more likely to find the items that have been neglected, ensuring that the agreement reached is equitable, reasonable, and workable. Having both dealt with the couple, co-mediators have had a firsthand opportunity to gather information about the couple's background and to develop impressions about how the couple functions and what, in the mind of each mediator, would be an equitable and workable solution. The mediators then confer to formulate directions and approaches to facilitate working with a particular couple.

Of greatest importance is the use of co-mediation as a quality control device. The importance of being observed within a clinical setting and obtaining quick and immediate feedback with regard to biases, prejudices, or procedural deviations cannot be overemphasized. It is easy for an individual, working alone without regular access to this kind of feedback, to slip into a set of behaviors or develop patterns of perceptions and responses that prohibit a neutral, equitable stance. Co-mediation provides this kind of quality control feedback to mediators, helping to prevent the type of deviation noted. Clearly, co-mediators can offer each other constructive criticism regarding behaviors, approaches, interpretations, and procedures in a way that improves the mediating skills of both mediators.

The co-mediation team is not always an equal partnership in terms of experience and professional qualifications. Co-mediation is an excellent procedure for training new mediators and providing experience to those who have not previously been directly involved in the mediation process. Many individuals feel that, by virtue of their previous professional training (e.g., in law, mental health, or negotiation), they have the skills in personal interaction and the experience necessary to conduct a mediation immediately. Mediation requires different skills, or skills in addition to those that the lawyer, therapist, or negotiator may have used before. Through the use of co-mediation, a less experienced mediator can observe firsthand and participate firsthand in a co-mediation process without jeopardizing the outcome for the couple because of the mediator's lack of experience. Even when no supervisor or experienced co-mediator is available, a newly trained mediator may join with another novice mediator, again, to learn by their mutual experience and to provide the checks, balances, and support that co-mediation offers.

Finally, Silberman (1982) viewed the interdisciplinary team as an answer to those who expressed concern that a nonlawyer mediator may be practicing law without authorization. Silberman also noted a problem with interdisciplinary co-mediation, however: "a lawyer cannot practice law in association with or in partnership with a nonlawyer and cannot split fees with a nonlawyer" (p. 261).

CONS

Some professionals feel that the number of people involved in co-mediation makes the dialogue/communication process too cumbersome. Their concern is that too many people will be trying to talk at once, or each will be trying to move in a different direction. After all, the channels of communication jump from 6 to 12 when the second mediator is added.

A co-mediator may have less control of the mediation process, since the other mediator must concur in actions taken; there is less spontaneity when the direction can be changed only by joint agreement. Again, there is a concern that two mediators, each with an agenda and a theory about which direction the process should go, may feel somewhat impotent. In addition, co-mediators are sometimes concerned about stepping on each other's toes or usurping control of the interaction or the communication. Some mediators reject the idea of co-mediation because of their own feelings of insecurity. They do not wish to be seen by others for fear of being condemned or criticized.

At another level, one of the most common questions about co-mediation is whether the couple should be penalized or charged an additional amount for co-mediation. This question has been dealt with in various ways. In some cases, the pros and cons have been explained, including the relative fee schedules, and the couple has been given the option of using a second mediator. Some agencies and private mediators simply charge twice the amount charged for a single mediator, while others make a 50% surcharge, or some other set figure, for a second mediator. The fee really should depend a great deal on the reason that a co-mediation team is being used. If co-mediation is presented as the "standard practice," the fees should be set as seems appropriate. If co-mediation is offered as an option, the agency providing that option should decide whether the couple is to be charged some additional amount for the second mediator. If the purpose of the co-mediation is to provide new mediators with experience or to evaluate quality, the mediators must consider their fee schedule carefully and decide whether the couple should, in fact, bear the brunt of their learning process.

Other professionals believe that co-mediation is an inefficient use of professional time. They feel that, since research shows that mediation by a single mediator is as effective as co-mediation, more people can be served in mediation if more mediators are free to mediate. Finally, from a very practical standpoint, the coordination of four calendars (especially when the couple is already separated and beginning independent activities) is considerably more difficult than is the coordination of three (which is not easy).

TECHNIQUES

One of the most often mentioned benefits of co-mediation is that of modeling. The co-mediators interact with each other in a mature and rational way, modeling the type of behavior that they hope to see from the couple. It is not necessary for them to be in complete agreement in every area, but when there is disagreement, they discuss the disagreement rationally and come to a compromise decision. They both accept the fact that they do not agree on a particular point. Similarly, it may sometimes be appropriate for them to model the behavior of the couple. The mediators may begin to fight or argue between themselves (preplanned) in order to demonstrate to the couple how they appear to others. This is most likely to be effective with hostile, aggressive couples, and it is usually demonstrated before it is explained to the couple.

In certain cases, it is appropriate for a mediator to form a temporary coalition with one spouse, supporting that spouse and empowering him or her to make a decision. In other situations, each mediator may temporarily join with one of the spouses, again to empower the couple to make decisions. The mediators must neither make decisions for the couple nor force the couple in one direction, however. The co-mediators may discuss and model strategies for communication, instead of just providing the physical model. The mediators can point out various communication strategies and indicate how they can be effective. Although this can obviously be described by one mediator, it is difficult for a single mediator to demonstrate.

Time-outs are effective in the mediation process. Often used by mediators and other professionals in helping clients, time-outs in a co-mediation setting not only allow the clients to relax and refocus, but also allow the co-mediators to discuss various strategies and approaches to use in dealing with the couple when they begin again.

When one or both spouses become intractable and will not move from a particular position, the co-mediators can take on the ''Mutt and Jeff'' or ''Good Guy-Bad Guy'' mantles. With this approach, the mediator who is the bad guy may become more argumentative, while the other mediator remains in the background, but ready to step in if necessary. An alternate approach is to have one mediator take an apparently entrenched position on a particular subject and then, after dealing with the other mediator for some time, begin to change his or her position. In this way, the mediators demonstrate a change of position on a particular topic without loss of face.

Co-mediators may set up a series of signals, either in words or behaviors, to indicate how they want to operate with each other on a particular issue. Taking off and putting on glasses, for example, may indicate ''I want to follow this line of discussion'' when the other mediator tries to intervene, or crossing the legs may indicate ''I am bailing out; take over for a while.'' Other signals may indicate ''Let's take a time-out and talk,'' ''Change the subject,'' or ''Help, I'm lost.'' Care must be taken not to make the signals too complex, or the mediators will spend more time looking at each other than at the couple.

It is not unusual in mediation proceedings for one spouse to focus frustrations and anger on a mediator rather than turning these feelings inward or sideways to the other spouse. When this happens in co-mediation, the anger can be diffused either by letting the mediator who is not the focus of that anger take over and direct the communications for a while or by asking why the client is focusing on just one mediator. In addition, the technique of distraction can be used to turn the angered or frustrated spouse away from the mediator who is receiving the brunt of attention.

REFERENCES

Black, M., & Joffee, W. (1978). A lawyer/therapist approach to divorce. *Conciliation Courts Review, 16*, 1–15.

Brown, D. (1982). Divorce and family mediation: History, review, future directions. *Conciliation Courts Review, 20*(2).

Coogler, O.J. (1978). *Structured mediation in divorce settlement: A handbook for marital mediators.* Lexington, MA: D.C. Heath.

Folberg, H.J. (1982). Divorce mediation: A workable alternative. *Alternative means of dispute resolution*, pp. 11–41. Washington, DC: ABA.

Freberg, H.J. (1981). Divorce mediation: A preliminary perspective. Reported by D. Brown (1982). Divorce and family mediation: History, review, future directions. *Conciliation Courts Review, 20*(2).

Gaybrick, A., & Bryner, D. (1981). Mediation in a public setting: Arlington, VA. *Family Law Reporting, 7*, 2390.

Gold, L. (1982). The psychological context of the interdisciplinary co-mediation team model in marital disolution. *Conciliation Courts Review, 20*(2).

Haynes, J.M. (1981). *Divorce mediation.* New York: Springer.

Nichols, R.E., & Troester, J.D. (1979). Custody evaluations: An alternative? *Family Coordinator, 28*, 399–407.

Silberman, L. (1982). Professional responsibility problems of divorce mediation. *Alternative Means of Dispute Resolution.* Washington, DC: ABA.

Wiseman, J., & Fiske, J. (1980). A lawyer therapist team as mediator in marital crisis. *Social Work, 25*, 442–445.

Wyckoff, R.B., & Cleveland, M. (1980). Custody resolution counseling: The Hennepin County alternative. Unpublished paper. Reported by D. Brown (1982). Divorce and family mediation: History, review, future directions. *Conciliation Courts Review, 20*(2).

7. Emotional Dynamics of Couples in Mediation

Emily M. Brown

Success in mediation depends as much on the mediator's ability to work with the emotional dynamics of the situation as on technical competency. The mediator must be able to identify significant emotional factors early in the process so as to select those interventions that are most likely to lead to resolution of the issues. Both situational and personality factors must be considered.

INITIAL INTERVIEW

Couples begin the process of divorce mediation at one of the most difficult times in their lives—immediately before or after separation. This is the most traumatic point in the entire divorce process. Massive disruption occurs, and grief is the overriding emotion. "Fight or flight" feelings are common. As if that were not enough, separation often stirs up unresolved issues from the past. The couple arrives at the mediator's office following an extended period of turmoil and pain. Since their behavior and communication patterns have proved insufficient to resolve the marital differences, they wonder whether mediation can be successful. The end result is a couple under stress and duress—not conducive to Emily Post behavior or to optimum functioning.

The mediator should first provide comfort. Some of this needs to be verbal, but much is nonverbal. The initial tone is set by the physical comfort provided by the office, which should be attractive, be furnished with comfortable chairs, and have an aura of calm. A helpful receptionist, a pleasant view, and coffee add to the couple's comfort.

Mediators themselves have more influence than is sometimes recognized, and small matters carry great weight. The clients' first impression of a mediator is based on social courtesies, such as whether the mediator is on time, welcomes each spouse, checks preferred names, attends to seating arrangements, and is attentive to each spouse. A moment of light conversation at the beginning gives the couple an opportunity to take measure of the mediator and the setting before they reveal highly personal information.

When the spouses have been through a long, difficult period with each other, as they have by the time they come to mediation, they find it reassuring to have the mediator take charge of the communication. The mediator needs to both tell the couple and demonstrate to them that he or she is in charge (Kelly, 1983). Ironically, when the spouses feel that the mediator is in control, they often give up some of their attempts to control. A small and carefully controlled release of feelings can relieve some of the pressure when the spouses have held in their feelings. If the release is too great, however, the couple will become frightened and back away from mediation. Humor is often a wonderful tool to use here. It offers the couple a shared experience, but establishes boundaries at the same time. Obviously, release of feelings is not to be encouraged with couples who come in swinging.

It is important for the mediator to know—and for the couples to know that the mediator knows—who is leaving whom. The "story" provides this information, as well as a host of other useful data. The storytelling usually comes early in the initial mediation session. Actually, there are two stories, which may or may not be similar; the mediator needs to hear each, while setting limits on how they are told. The storytelling, in both its style and its content, helps the mediator to get to know the marital partners as individuals and to hear their concerns, their priorities, their fears, and their hurts. It provides an opportunity for the husband and wife each to be heard and accepted as individuals. This is an important step in laying the groundwork for the later negotiations.

While the "story" is especially useful, everything that happens in the initial session (and in subsequent sessions) can be used by the mediator to identify emotional factors that will affect the process of mediation. Careful observation of communication patterns and emotional vibrations, combined with information provided by the couple, gives the mediator a good reading on where the difficulties will lie. A checklist is helpful in facilitating the assessment process (Exhibit 7–1).

THE DECISION TO DIVORCE

For some couples, the decision to divorce (or separate) marks a real change in the relationship; for others, it is the latest escalation of business as usual. The meaning depends on whether the decision reflects growth or avoidance on the part of one or both spouses in dealing with their personal and marital problems. Marris (1974) went to the heart of avoidance when he stated that "to revise the principles by which we have interpreted the past is a far more arduous and impenetrable task than to make what happens now conform to them" (p. 14).

Mediating couples can be divided into three categories: those in which growth is a factor for both partners, those in which avoidance is a factor for both, and those in which one spouse has grown—and outgrown—the other.

Exhibit 7–1 Orientation Session: Assessment Checklist

1. Data Collection
   Initiator/noninitiator
   Stated reasons for divorce
   Marital history (cooperation, conflict, or avoidance)
   Parenting roles
   Third parties
   Content of communication
      cooperation
      blaming
      complaining
      hostility
      ambiguity
   Focus of attention/conflict
2. Observation
   Communication style
      who speaks for whom
      who speaks to whom
      pattern of interruptions
      balance
      perseverance/avoidance
      zingers
   Predominant affect of each
3. Inference
   Real reasons for divorce
   Emotional hot spots
   Level of good will

The decision to divorce results from the growth of both partners in only a small number of cases. The incidence may be low because such growth leads more often to a continuance of the marriage than to separation. When these couples do come to mediation, they are more likely to have accepted the separation, have a greater ability to stay task-oriented, and exhibit fewer emotional outbursts. The emotional tone tends to be one of rationality mixed with sadness, of resignation punctuated occasionally by pointed remarks. This pattern is roughly analogous to the pattern of disengaged conflict described by Kressel, Jaffe, Tuchman, Watson, and Deutsch (1980) in their study of a very small sample of couples who used mediation to negotiate the terms of their separation agreements. These researchers noted low levels of ambivalence, communication, and conflict with these couples.

Avoidance

A significant factor for at least one partner in most dissolving marriages is avoidance. When only one spouse is an avoider, the avoidance surfaces in mediation as an unwillingness to raise issues or make demands. The unwillingness is often disguised as concern for the spouse's feelings, such as "I don't want to upset her," or as helplessness, such as "I don't know how." Anger is another manifestation of avoidance; for example, the wife may say, "He's the one who wants out—I don't know why I should have to suffer when he's doing what he wants!" Some of the anger is situational, but some is more basic, reflecting the avoider's dislike for having to deal with painful realities. Illumination and acceptance by the mediator of such feelings must precede a decision to mediate (Blades, 1984).

Avoiders are not accustomed to handling their own lives and may need extra help from the mediator to do so. At the same time, the mediator must be careful not to be seduced into doing too much for the avoider or into neglecting the other spouse, who is likely to be disgusted, if not enraged, by the avoidance if it persists. The mediator must intervene to prevent the other spouse from making attacks or disparaging remarks, which will only encourage further avoidance. With an avoider, the mediator must be very firm and very specific in assigning tasks. It is essential to obtain a commitment for the performance of the task. If the avoider does not perform as agreed, the mediator can

1. choose not to proceed with mediation until the task is completed. This strategy is not successful if the avoider's goal is to delay or prevent separation or divorce, however. It is more effective with "nice guy" (or gal) types than with helpless types.
2. proceed, using the existing information. This often spurs the helpless types into action, but it must be done carefully so as to avoid the appearance of taking the side of the other spouse.
3. give the avoider the responsibility for deciding how to proceed, given the uncompleted task. If the avoider plays a hard game of "wooden leg" or "I'm only trying to help you" (Berne, 1964), or refuses responsibility in other ways, this is the best strategy.

In a significant number of divorcing couples, both partners have avoided dealing with the marital problems, and one chooses divorce as a way to continue avoiding. With the easing of divorce laws, this group seems to be growing. Couples in which both are avoiders may be quiet or contentious, but they are difficult to deal with in mediation; an infinite number of games may be played. The surface manifestations include model behavior, double messages and expressions of ambivalence, or fights over small and irrelevant matters. Model behavior is commonly seen in remarks such as ''See how civilized we are,'' ''Let's just get it over with,'' or ''You know what's best—just tell us what to do.'' The need to avoid guilt, pain, obstacles to separation, or personal demons is so strong that they prefer not to discuss matters fully; they just want to make a decision and run. If allowed to do so, however, relitigation is likely. Interventions must emphasize clear and complete communication, as well as ''I'' messages. The mediator should use a deliberate style and resist the invitations to slide over certain matters or to rush the process. When games are mild and the couple seems highly ambivalent, there is a possibility of reconciliation, which should be explored. Spouses who are receptive to the idea of reconciliation should be referred for marital therapy.

The hard game players are often more interested in proving their point and getting their payoff than in reaching agreement. The contentiousness is not an aspect of the normal grief process, but has deeper and more longstanding roots. It is a way of coping with unresolved losses from the past. Although the issues and coping strategies began as individual ones, the spouses play reciprocal roles and reinforce each other's behavior.

With such couples, it is more important than ever that the mediator stay in control of the communication, insisting on ''I'' messages and avoiding the traps laid to entice him or her into the role of judge. Redirecting the focus to a shared concern can be useful, as can reframing the issue so as to touch on the strengths of either spouse. Black humor, such as alluding to their agreement to dislike each other, can defuse some of the rancor. Patrician (1984) suggested pursuing secondary goals with these couples, in part for their paradoxical effect. Saposnek's (1983) strategy of leaving the room can also be quite effective. He tells the couple that he is not interested in listening to them argue, but instructs them to continue and to let him know when they have finished and are ready for mediation, and he leaves. In the interest of self-preservation, the mediator must allow ample time for recovery after a session with these couples.

Findings from the Denver Mediation Project (Pearson & Thoennes, 1984) indicate that mediation is most important for those with some emotional conflict. Mediation is inappropriate, however, for those with a long history of formal grievances or litigation. Therapy is usually necessary to change such behavior patterns, but it is rarely undertaken voluntarily. Mediators may be most helpful to these families by recommending that they undergo therapy or, if in a position to do so, by recommending that the court so order. Since these spouses always deny that they need therapy, the recommendation needs to be framed in a way that facilitates the couple's acceptance.

The underutilization of mediation (Pearson & Thoennes, 1984) may be due to the large number of avoiders in the divorcing population. It seems likely that many avoiders would prefer to have someone else handle their divorce for them.

Emotional Maturity

Closely related to personal growth, emotional maturity is inversely correlated with the intensity of game playing in mediation. Maturity is defined here as the acceptance of the imperfections of the world, together with the relinquishment of the fantasy of finding someone else to handle the responsibilities of life. Spouses with emotional maturity do not hold each other hostage for not having been a good enough spouse (or parent), and it is unlikely that there will be fireworks in mediation with such a couple. In contrast, spouses who are immature will use strong-arm tactics in a last-ditch effort to get the other to give them what they want. They may threaten the spouse or even the mediator. These are not really threats, but tantrums. The mediator must avoid taking a parental role and direct interventions toward the most mature part of the person. Conversely, permission to have a tantrum (i.e., "You can choose to leave if that is what you want to do ") sometimes takes all the fun out of this maneuver.

Younger couples without children are less likely to cling to their marriage than are couples who have invested more in the marriage and whose habits are of many years' duration. The young are also more able and willing to begin again. Ownership of property usually brings these couples to mediation, and the most likely pitfall is for one or the other to give up everything in the rush to become "free."

The "Dumper/Dumpee" Factor

The decision to divorce is rarely a mutual one, and much of the emotional intensity associated with divorce can be attributed to this fact. Usually, the decision is made unilaterally, and the noninitiating spouse (the "dumpee" in the vernacular) is one of the last to know about it (Brown, 1976). Sometimes, one spouse forces the other to take responsibility for the decision, although unwittingly or even unconsciously. It is quite common for a "dumpee" to admit a year or so later that he or she was miserable in the marriage but was unable to confront the situation. In any case, the partners are out of phase with each other for a great part of the divorce process, particularly at the time of separation, when mediation commonly takes place (Figure 7–1). The initiator has completed some of the grief work and is better able to focus on the issues at hand. The noninitiator is not only thrust

---

Figure 7–1 Steps in the Emotional Process of Divorce

Initiator		*Noninitiator*
Deny problems/possibility of split		Deny problems/possibility of split
Consider possibility of separation	**Decision-making Phase**	
Anger and blame		
Loss, grief, and helplessness		
Guilt and failure		
Detachment		
Decision		
Separation	End of Marriage	Separation
Cope with massive change in living patterns	*Marriage still primary reference point*	Acknowledge fact of separation
		Anger and blame
Develop new social relationships		Loss, grief, and helplessness
Explore new opportunities and challenges		Guilt and failure
		Manage day-to-day activities
Understand marital breakdown, including own contribution		Implement small decisions
		Develop new social relationships
Accept responsibility for own actions	**Restructuring Phase**	Accept separation/divorce
Reassess values and needs		Explore new opportunities and challenges
Set long-term goals		Understand marital breakdown, including own contribution
Develop autonomy		
		Accept responsibility for own actions
	Marriage not primary reference point	Reassess values and needs
		Set long-term goals
		Develop autonomy

*Mediation generally takes place during this phase of the divorce process.

Source: E.M. Brown (1976). A model of the divorce process. *Conciliation Courts Review 14(2).* Copyright © 1976 by Emily M. Brown. Reprinted by permission.

into the grief process, but also is required simultaneously to deal with the practical issues of separation.

Since guilt, anger, and denial are aspects of grief, the mediator can expect these feelings to surface, particularly in the "dumpee." The "dumper," while further along, has not yet completed the grief process and may express similar feelings. In addition, the "dumper" may resonate to the "dumpee's" expressions of anger. Thus, mediation is loaded with intense and difficult feelings, the expression of which is often loud.

When one partner has grown and the other has not, mediation is more difficult than it is when both partners have grown. In these one-sided situations, the person who has grown becomes the "dumper," while the "dumpee" hangs on for dear life. The desperation shows in the "dumpee's" refusal to consider options, denial of any responsibility for the marital difficulties, hostile remarks, and attempts to obtain concessions by establishing the "dumper's" guilt.

The noninitiator is in a one-down position, feeling somewhat bloodied and powerless. When power cannot be regained by direct attempts, passive strategies will be used. Bowlby's description of the grief process (1961) is apropos:

> So long as the response systems are focused on the lost object there are strenuous and often angry efforts to recover it; and these efforts may continue despite their fruitlessness being painfully evident to others and sometimes also to the bereaved himself. (p. 319)

Depending on the interaction pattern, the noninitiator in this situation may play the martyr, be passive to the point of sabotage, exact punishment, or look to a gladiator. The mediator must take a strong hand in managing the communication, ruling out of order any attempts to attack or blame, while encouraging and supporting the noninitiator in making proposals.

Third Parties

In some instances, one spouse is involved in a new love relationship before the separation. By definition, the spouse so involved has avoided dealing with the marital problems. The other spouse may or may not be an avoider, but this escalation of events makes it impossible for the "wronged" spouse to continue avoiding.

If the affair has been a brief fling, the marriage may not be over. The affair of long standing, particularly when the involved spouse has moved from the marital household to the lover's household, is another matter entirely. Couples in this type of situation have generally invested a good deal of time in each other (8 to 10 years or more) and often have children. The romance of an affair may sufficiently obscure the guilt arising from the presence of the children to allow the spouse to leave. In this situation, it is usually the husband who is the "dumper." It is not clear whether this is because women tend to be more involved with the children and have fewer financial resources or whether it is for other reasons.

Mediation commonly takes place shortly after the discovery of the affair, before the betrayed spouse has had a chance to come to terms with the situation and his or her own role in it. Expressions of grief are stronger when betrayal is a factor. Enormous anger, which often seems excessive even to the one betrayed, may be projected into other facets of mediation. Parenting arrangements are a common target, and punishment may be veiled as an attempt to protect the children. Anger and the desire for retribution are also played out over money and property.

Slowing down the mediation process allows the betrayed partner time to recover from the shock, consider needs and priorities, and move into a position from which to negotiate. In many cases, the first request made by this spouse is for time, and most often the other spouse readily agrees. The spouse who is "dumped" in this manner often welcomes a referral for therapy; this is best done early in the mediation process. A shift from tears to anger on the part of the "dumpee" is healthy and indicates increased ability to negotiate in his or her own behalf. The "dumper" often tries to appease the guilt by making unrealistic offers. It is not uncommon for a guilty husband to offer his wife the house, the car, and the greater share of the other assets, plus most of his income in support. If these offers were accepted, the husband would be unable to function. It is the mediator's job to point out the unrealistic nature of these offers and to help both spouses focus on the realities of their situation and their shared concerns.

INTERACTION STYLES: CHILDREN AS A CASE IN POINT

Cooperation, conflict, and avoidance are the major styles that couples use in mediation. Some couples consistently use one style, while others may use different styles to deal with different issues. The greatest intensity of feeling, no matter what the style, is often shown in the discussion of parenting arrangements. Although this discussion focuses on parenting arrangements, it applies also to the way in which other issues are mediated.

The presence of children in a marriage brings an additional dimension to divorce. Children can become the primary reason for cooperation, the trophy awarded for defeating the opponent, or a responsibility to be avoided. Which of these is true depends on the parents' predominant way of dealing with each other and on their level of maturity. The mediator cannot change the parents' basic orientation, but must channel its expression.

Parenting arrangements are easy to design with parents who are able to cooperate in behalf of their children. The mediator's function in this case is primarily to provide information about options and to raise issues that the parents need to consider. If the parents are considering an alternating days arrangement, for example, the mediator might question the children's ability to tolerate the constant change, share problems that other parents have had with this arrangement, or suggest other uses for this parental energy.

When one parent declines responsibility for the children, it is usually because that parent is unable to put the children's needs ahead of his or her own. He or she (still usually he) may find it too painful, too time-consuming, or too uncomfortable to deal with the frequent goodbyes. In some cases, the mediator can help a father understand the important role that he can play with his children. Discussing ways to minimize any impediments can also help. If, for example, some of the discomfort comes from seeing the mother's boyfriend, the pickup and dropoff arrangements might be modi- fied. When one spouse is reluctant to accept his or her parental responsibil- ity, the mediator must ensure that the visitation arrangements are very specific, since undefined arrangements have a way of encouraging pro- crastination and avoidance.

Mediation is most difficult with couples who are immature and unable to keep their personal feelings separate from their parental roles. Their fight over the children is motivated by bitterness, the desire for revenge, or the wish to be vindicated. When revenge is the primary motivation, it is extremely important for the mediator to set limits. The mediator must combine authority with sensitivity to the clients' emotional vulnerability lurking just under the surface. Since people respond best when their feelings are accepted and their best selves challenged, the mediator should acknowl- edge the anger, but make it clear that positive behavior is expected. Redirec- tion and appeals to other motivators are also useful.

It is a little easier to deal with the wish to be vindicated. This is commonly seen with women who have invested their entire lives in being wives and mothers. Divorce causes them to lose a significant part of their identity, and they may cling to the remainder, the mother role, by clinging to the children. Derdeyn and Scott (1984) described grief as similar to suspense, because in both there is a frustration of many impulses that have become habitual. "The desire to have custody of children may be driven by the same dreadful sense of disorientation. If one can keep one's children, one can better maintain one's sense of purpose and of continuity in the parental identity" (p. 205).

The wish to be vindicated can also be fueled by self-doubt or by guilt, which may or may not have anything to do with parenting. While long-term solutions require the spouses to adopt new roles, the mediation process can be facilitated by helping the spouses vindicate each other. To do this, the mediator must help the spouses identify exactly what they want from the other spouse in the way of vindication. The wife, for example, may want her husband to acknowledge that she was a good wife during the earlier part of the marriage. He, in turn, may want her to acknowledge that he worked hard to be a good provider. If the desired acknowledgement has been correctly identified (and precision here is important) and honestly given, this technique may end the unproductive conflict. No longer needing vindication and with whatever good will has been generated by the acknowledgement of past efforts, they can begin to work on present issues.

SPECIAL PROBLEMS

Mediators, particularly those with training in mental health, are sometimes asked to mediate cases that are particularly problematic. Divorces involving an alcoholic or mentally ill spouse may be appropriate for therapy, but not for mediation. The other spouse, having tolerated the situation for many years, is finally ready to dump the problem spouse, often into an institution. The martyred spouse, usually a man in this scenario, is likely to view the joint property as his alone because the wife is incompetent. Unless fully able to negotiate, the ill spouse needs the protection of an advocate. The mediator should refer both spouses to competent and responsible attorneys.

NURTURING

Because of the immense sense of loss, divorcing spouses have a tremendous need for nurturing. At the same time, they often behave in ways that do not endear them to the mediator. The temper tantrum in a mediation client is much like that in the 4-year-old and can be handled similarly. Holding the 4-year-old stops the behavior, while conveying a human connection. The mediation client also needs firm limits and human connection, although not necessarily in the same form. A pat on the shoulder or a touch on the knee of a client who feels isolated can be tremendously effective, even when the verbal message is to be quiet.

Mediators need to determine the ways in which they are comfortable nurturing clients. Some mediators find that verbal strokes alone are sufficient, while others may choose to touch, to offer coffee, or to comfort their clients in other ways. Touching should never be used with clients who are overly suspicious or who repeatedly question the motives of others, nor in any situation in which it could be interpreted as a sexual overture. The biggest danger in comforting clients is that it may reinforce dependent behavior, however. In nurturing, the mediator should convey the message that "I know you're in a tough spot, and I feel for your pain; but the only way to feel better is to face this, so let's get at it."

CONCLUSION

Although each couple in mediation is different, there are common patterns of behavior. Several factors are clues to the meaning of the behavior. The goal of assessment is to develop an overall picture that can be used as a guide in selecting interventions. Sharp delineation of detail is not necessary. Rather, by identifying patterns of behavior and the underlying motivations, the mediator can select interventions to modify or prevent the occurrence of dysfunctional behaviors and to encourage the emergence of strengths and cooperative behaviors.

REFERENCES

Berne, E. (1964). *Games people play*. New York: Grove Press.

Blades, J. (1984). Mediation: An old art revitalized. *Mediation Quarterly, 1*(3), 59–98.

Bowlby, J. (1961). Process of mourning. *International Journal of Psychoanalysis, 42*(4/5), 319–320.

Brown, E.M. (1976). A model of the divorce process. *Conciliation Courts Review, 14*(2), 1–11.

Derdeyn, A.P., & Scott, E. (1984). Joint custody: A critical analysis and appraisal. *American Journal of Orthopsychiatry, 54*(2), 199–209.

Kelly, J.B. (1983). Mediation and psychotherapy: Distinguishing the differences. *Mediation Quarterly, 1*(1), 33–44.

Kressel, K., Jaffe, N., Tuchman, B., Watson, C., & Deutsch, M. (1980). A typology of divorcing couples: Implications for mediation and the divorce process. *Family Process, 19*(2), 101–116.

Marris, P. (1974). *Loss and change.* New York: Doubleday.

Patrician, M. (1984). Situation mediation. *Conciliation Courts Review, 22*(1), 75–80.

Pearson, J., & Thoennes, N. (1984). Mediating and litigating custody disputes: A longitudinal evaluation. *Family Law Quarterly, 17*(4), 497–517.

Saposnek, D.T. (1983). Strategies in child custody mediation: A family systems approach. *Mediation Quarterly, 1*(2), 29–54.

8. Including Children in Mediation: Considerations for the Mediator

Karen K. Irvin

Many PROFESSIONALS CURRENTLY WORKING IN THE FIELD OF DIVORCE counseling have become aware of mediation as an alternative for couples and families in the dissolution process. Several authors have addressed the practice of family mediation (e.g., Coogler, 1978; Haynes, 1981); others have specifically addressed "custody" mediation (e.g., Cleveland & Irvin, 1982; Saposnek, 1983). Very little attention has been paid to actually including children in mediation sessions and/or interviewing them as part of the mediation process, however. In essence, those most directly affected by the custody decisions are omitted from the decision-making process.

BEFORE ATTEMPTING CUSTODY MEDIATION

If a mediator is to work directly with children, with or without their parents present, some specific knowledge is needed.

Developmental Stages and Needs of Children

Perhaps the most basic knowledge that a mediator requires to work directly with children is a knowledge of their developmental needs and the ways in which these needs may be affected by the divorce process. If children are to be included in sessions, the mediator must adapt the time and length of sessions, vocabulary, use of abstract concepts (e.g., "divorce"), furnishings and supplies available, and even the layout of the office to their developmental level (Zilbach, 1982). Four-year-olds do not sit and talk quietly for 2 hours, adolescents often have a unique vocabulary, and all children need some space to escape from tension and anxiety during a session.

The mediator's knowledge of children's developmental needs is also helpful to parents, who often look to the mediator for information about their children's reactions to the divorce. They wonder whether their children are "just going through a stage" or whether specific behaviors are related to the divorce. They ask about the implications of the various options for scheduling time with their children. The mediator can be a useful resource for parents as they make the decisions that affect their children. The mediator should also be able to refer parents to books and professionals who further address parents' questions and concerns.

Custody mediation should include mention of the prospective needs of adult children. Parents tend to believe that, once their children reach age 18, they no longer need to interact as parents. However, divorced parents should anticipate college graduations, weddings, grandchildren, and other occasions that might continue to bring them together to meet the needs of their children.

The Divorce Process: Emotional and Legal

Several models have been proposed to define the emotional process of divorce for adults, and some apply just as readily to children experiencing divorce. Certainly, a basic grief model of denial, anger, depression, bargaining, and acceptance applies to children experiencing family change as well as to adults. Whether using this model or others, such as those proposed by Bohannan or Kessler (cited in Kaslow, 1981), the mediator must understand the impact on both adults and children.

In order to assist the family as much as possible, the mediator must be able to anticipate the emotional implications of the mediation process for each member of the family. For example, the person making the decision to leave the relationship is apt to be ready to make decisions "rationally," while the other partner may still be caught in the denial and anger, and may make proposals that do not seem "rational." To the extent that parents are negotiating custody, the mediator should help them understand both their own and the other's views and proposals as well as the motivation for each. It is also helpful to explain to children in the mediation process the emotional process for both parents and children.

The mediator should also understand the legal process of dissolution and the ways in which it may affect the family and its negotiations. Some families have not as yet consulted an attorney and have no idea what will happen when they do. They may ask for explanations from the mediator. Others may have begun the legal process, but may be unaware of the potential impact of some aspects of it, such as the service of a summons and petition. An objective explanation of any aspect of the legal processes can be very helpful and supportive to all family members. In *The Kids' Book of Divorce* (1981), for example, Rofes provided an anecdotal, understandable explanation of this process for children. The mediator may find it helpful to attend a few hearings and litigated proceedings in order to understand those processes and appreciate the clients' experiences in them. The mediator can also learn about the idiosyncrasies of local courts and judges, particularly as they apply to custody options.

Although a mediator need not have the knowledge of statutes expected of legal counsel, statutes are discussed in mediation. Both children and adults often inquire about the age at which children can legally choose a custodial parent. Statutes often contain definitions of joint custody and mediation expectations or requirements that families may want to incorporate into their agreements. A guardian ad litem might be involved. In general, it is useful for mediators to be acquainted with mediation, custody, and visitation statutes in their jurisdiction.

Research

Mediators who work with custody issues and/or children must keep abreast of developments in the field of mediation as well as in the field of divorce. There has been a tremendous surge in these vital areas of research over the past 10 years, and it is likely to continue as divorce is accepted in American society. Efforts to study divorce mediation, such as those at the Denver Research Project (Pearson, Ring & Milne, 1983), continue to provide information relative to the mediation process. The effects of divorce on children (Wallerstein & Kelly, 1980) and the success of various custody options (Ahrons, 1980) have also become important areas of research. Mediators must incorporate the findings of such research into their practice.

BEFORE INCLUDING CHILDREN

Once custody has been identified as an issue for mediation, the best way to include children in the mediation process must be determined. Berg (1983) stated that "mediation gives a golden opportunity to do right by the children" (p. 28) and recommended that mediators see children personally, if necessary. Haynes (1981) described children in mediation as "less than equal partners to make sure they understand the reason for the divorce, the permanence of the decision, and the neutrality of their roles in the decision of parents to divorce" (p. 134). He speculated that once they are informed, they are better able to express their wishes, concerns, and fears and thereby to enter the negotiation process with their parents. Coulson (1983) substantially agreed.

Vanderkooi and Pearson (1983) described mediation as a

> cooperative resolution process in which a neutral intervenor helps disputing parties negotiate a mutually satisfactory settlement of their conflict. The process stresses honesty, informality, open and direct communication, emotional expressiveness, attention to underlying causes of disputes, reinforcement of positive bonds and avoidance of blame. (p. 557)

Although children may not fall into the category of "disputing parties," there are benefits to be gained by allowing them to observe and participate in negotiation sessions. For many children, this may be the first time in months or years that they actually observe these dynamics between their parents. When the children understand that one of the primary motivations for the parents' mediating is their love and concern for them, it can be very supportive for the children.

Another advantage of having children present during mediation is the potential for positive reinforcement for the existing parenting and caring relationships. For example, a toddler at play during a mediation session brought a variety of items to his mother and his father in turn, giving and getting affection from each. This provided the mediator with an opportunity to observe and indicate to the parents how comfortable this child was with both and to commend them for their nurturance of the child's attachment to both parents.

Finally, children's concerns tend to be somewhat more concrete and immediate than those of their parents. They want to know which toys will be in which house, which furniture will be moved, and the exact day and hour that the moves will be made. Their presence in mediation allows them to express these questions and concerns and receive direct responses from parents.

Including children in sessions also has potentially negative consequences. Parents sometimes express reluctance to expose children to their disagreements and hostility, as if the children who lived in the same household with those feelings for years have somehow been oblivious to them! Although the children may have their observations and feelings validated in mediation, and may hear that the parents intend to handle such feelings differently in the future, the existence of these feelings can make for highly volatile mediation sessions. It is undesirable to expose children to continued accusations, diatribes, and discord if the parents are not progressing toward settlement of the custody issues.

Children tend to display their feelings of sadness, anger, fear, and confusion openly. This can become a problem in mediation sessions if the mediator is unwilling or unable to respond to these feelings or if parents blame each other and/or the mediator for the children's emotions, claiming that the children are being traumatized. Although it is doubtful that the mediation session itself will traumatize the children, the mediator should be prepared to excuse the children or terminate the session if the parents' efforts to resolve issues are not constructive. The effects of such behavior on the children can be utilized in later sessions with the parents (without making them feel ashamed) to explain that their children's emotional needs must be addressed in conjunction with the custody negotiations. One of the primary hazards of not including children in the negotiations is that the children may be strongly opposed to arrangements that their parents have agreed are fair and reasonable. Although children should not have the final say in the custodial decisions, their input early in the process can avoid many problems.

The children of parents who seem to be intent on keeping children "in the middle" and using them as weapons, or those who are still steeped in anger and hostility, should not be allowed to participate in mediation. Children should also be excluded from sessions when both parents are reluctant to assume responsibility for them. In most custody disputes, both parents want their children; in a few, however, neither parent is committed to rearing the children. Finally, the mediator who is not comfortable and skillful in doing so should not include children in sessions. These mediators may

- limit their practice to those families with only property and financial issues
- utilize another service or mediator, such as court-connected services, for custody issues
- address the custody issues without including children in the sessions, still providing the parents with the information they require about the needs of children
- attempt to improve their skill and comfort level with children through further education and co-mediation with mediators who do include children

INCLUDING CHILDREN

Most mediators conduct at least a brief orientation in order to familiarize the couple with the mediation process and to familiarize themselves with the family and the issues to be addressed. Some mediators prefer that children participate from the beginning, including the orientation, if they are planning to include the children at all. It is their belief that children benefit from the explanation of the mediation process and that mediators benefit from getting acquainted with the children immediately. Other mediators prefer to meet with the parents alone during the orientation in order to determine with them the best time to include the children, if at all.

Children may be included in all the sessions, particularly if they are old enough to understand and participate in most of the discussions. Some mediators believe that the children have a vested interest in the entire process and like to be involved from beginning to end. They benefit from seeing their parents cooperate to resolve conflicts in many different areas of their lives. In addition, the children may have a stabilizing influence on the parents if they are parents who choose to keep hostility at a minimum when the children are present. According to Saposnek (1983), children can help to break impasses not only by offering suggestions, but also by asking their parents to stop fighting. Obviously, this technique is not without risks, and the mediator has the ethical responsibility to protect the children from excessive emotional pain while ensuring that the parents are aware of the children's feelings.

Another option is to include children in custody mediation sessions only. Mediators who prefer this option assume that the children are such an integral part of the custody negotiations that they should be included in those sessions. The children are encouraged to express ideas and feelings, to be creative, and to explore options with their parents; however, the parents are ultimately responsible for the decision.

Finally, children may be invited into the mediation process after the parents have reached all of the necessary agreements. The parents and/or the mediator then interpret the agreements to the children, answer any questions they might have about them, and provide positive support for moving forward with the restructuring process. This option places the children at minimal emotional risk, but it also minimizes the children's input into decisions.

Whenever children are included in mediation, it should be made clear that they will never be asked to choose between their parents and that the custody decision is not theirs to make. Parents must be supported in their decision-making efforts, with the children's input being appropriately considered.

Format for Including Children

There are several formats that may be used to include children in mediation sessions. Children may be seen with both parents, with only one parent at a time, as a sibling group, as individuals, or in any combination (Kantor & Vickers, 1983). Many mediators spend at least some time alone with the children in order to get acquainted, make the children comfortable, explain their role in the process, and hear the children's questions, ideas, and concerns. Before conducting these sessions, the mediator must clarify the ethical implications to the entire family. For instance, will information from the children be kept confidential? If the mediator is not willing to keep secrets, it is probably best not to separate segments of the family.

Children are apt to express themselves differently when seen alone than when seen with siblings. One sibling may be the spokesperson for the group, giving the others little opportunity to speak openly. One may be more shy, more introverted, or more frightened about the divorce, expressing few of his or her own ideas and echoing those of the other children. There is safety in numbers, however, particularly in a new situation. The children may feel more secure if the mediator sees them together at first. It is useful to consult with the parents and to ask the children themselves if they would like an opportunity to meet and talk alone, separately from the other children. Once permission is given to do so, many children enjoy having a few minutes alone to express their own opinions and concerns.

Including children in a mediation session with the parents provides the best opportunity for all participants to react to each other as questions are asked and statements made. It is also very useful in doing the diagnostic work (Kelly, 1983). If the mediator is not trained in family systems dynamics, however, it can be very confusing and overwhelming, particularly if done by a lone mediator.

Roles of Mediator with Children

Whether the children are interviewed with the parents or separately, the mediator plays a variety of roles for children:

- educator: to teach about the mediation process, the divorce process, the ways in which change affects people (both adults and children), and feelings associated with the process—all in an effort to normalize these dynamics for the children
- supporter: to encourage and understand ideas and feelings expressed by the children, and to emphasize some of the positives that are likely to or already have taken place in the family (e.g., less arguing, two birthday parties)
- confidant: to be willing to keep secret the fantasies, fears, preferences, ideas, and concerns that the children wish to be kept from their parents
- messenger: to take to the parents those things that the children would like for them to know but have not yet been able to express
- advocate: to assume the role of the children's protector in the event the parents are unable or unwilling to consider their best interests

- resource: to lead children to reading materials, plays, movies, professional resources in the school and community, other children, and legal resources, if needed
- evaluator: to determine whether the children appear to be adjusting to the separation and divorce in the context of their overall development
- therapist: to help children reestablish some sense of equilibrium, to focus at least temporarily on their feelings, and to improve family relationships

The last two of these roles may appear to be inappropriate for a mediator. Kelly (1983) indicated, however, that the present and future needs of all family members must be evaluated in mediation. To the extent that the children's needs can be identified and incorporated into the strategy for settlement, the mediator is facilitating custodial agreements for the family. This is not to suggest that these evaluations should be formalized as custody recommendations (to parents or courts), but rather they should be used to help parents understand their children's needs.

Some mediators assume the role of counselor or therapist when working with children—more so than with the parents. In custody resolution counseling (Cleveland & Irvin, 1982), the feelings of all family members are explored in some depth. If children are to be included (or interviewed separately), these feelings may be the focus of the sessions.

Mediators may opt to play some or all of these roles, depending on the mediation model that best suits them. The roles must be thoughtfully considered and carefully selected in advance, however, and the mediator must be clear about which will be utilized and why. The last thing families in the process of dissolution need is further confusion.

Techniques for Including Children

Most professionals who work with children have ways to make them comfortable so that the task at hand can be accomplished. For example, pediatricians have techniques for getting children to cooperate with physical examinations, as well as rewards for doing so. The same is true for teachers, therapists, and other children's professionals. Many of the same theories apply to children in mediation.

Children first must be prepared for the mediation sessions. Milne (1978) provided parents with specific facts to explain to children before the children participate in mediation:

- information about prior sessions with parents, if any
- examples of topics to be covered with the children
- the desire of the mediator to get acquainted with the children in order to be more helpful to the family
- assurance that the mediator will not ask the children to choose between Mom and Dad
- assurance that the parents will make the decision with the mediator's help

The mediator must take some time to get acquainted with the children. After the introductions, the mediator should ask questions that the children can answer easily, such as age, birth date, grade in school, which school, favorite subjects, pets, sports, or music. The purpose is to make the child comfortable. Humor is extremely helpful in meeting and working with children. It is also helpful to have some knowledge of the current heroes and heroines for the varying age groups, from Saturday morning cartoons to rock groups; to know something about current clothing fads (one mediator asked a 14-year-old if he had injured his wrist because he was wearing a bandanna wrapped around it, a current fad at the local high schools); and otherwise to be able to converse about items of interest to the children.

The next step is to clarify the purpose of the meeting. This can usually be accomplished by asking what Mom or Dad told them about coming to the meeting. Most children remember little, but usually something. It is then up to the mediator to clarify the purpose or to request that the parents do so if they are present for the interview. It is also important to use a vocabulary that is understandable to all the children present.

Discussion questions can then be asked (Bienenfeld, 1980):

- What are the current arrangements—when do you see Mom? Dad?
- How are those arrangements working?
- Do you know other kids whose parents do not live together?
- What kinds of things do you do with Dad? Mom?
- What kinds of things do you need from each?
- How do you get along with each parent? With brothers and sisters?
- How is school going?
- How much arguing and fighting is still going on?

- What do you do when it does happen? How do you feel?
- Any special worries or fears about Mom? About Dad?
- What is the best thing about Dad? About Mom?
- How do Mom and Dad punish you?
- Does your family take vacations? What do you do?
- What do you like to do with your friends?
- What sports do you like?
- Everyone is afraid of something—what are you afraid of?
- Do you have a job? An allowance? What do you do with the money?
- What would you wish for if you had three wishes?
- Is there anything I forgot to ask you? Anything you'd like to ask?

Mediators should avoid asking children loaded questions or questions for which they already have answers. They should also avoid complex sentences and questions. Questions preceded by "what if," "suppose that," or "let's pretend" can give a gamelike quality and prevent the children from feeling assaulted by the questions. Finally, it is important to pay attention to children's nonverbal, as well as to their verbal, responses.

ETHICAL CONSIDERATIONS

In the field of mediation, ethical considerations and standards of practice are currently receiving much attention. Including children in mediation raises several ethical questions. For example, who should make the decision to include the children in mediation sessions and/or to have them interviewed? Should mediators establish a model of mediation and present it as nonnegotiable? If it is a model that includes the children, should it specify the circumstances and timing for doing so? Or should parents be given that decision to make? Since parents are being encouraged to make decisions about all aspects of their lives in the mediation process, it seems that they should decide whether to include their children in the process. It is hoped that the decision would be based on adequate information about the pros and cons of including children.

The confidentiality of the information gained from the children in separate interviews must also be considered. How should the stated preferences of children be addressed, and how much weight should be given such preferences, particularly if stated in confidence? Similarly, what actions should mediators take based on impressions formed during interviews with the children? Are the children fearful of abandonment or of reprisal for wanting more contact with one parent? Are they trying to take care of or otherwise act as a companion to one parent? Do they appear hostile toward stepfamily members (Clawar, 1983)? The way in which such impressions will be handled should be determined and clarified with all parties before any interviews. If mediators are required to report child abuse or neglect, clients should be made aware of the implications for them in mediation. If children report abuse or neglect and the mediator is obligated to report to authorities, the mediation process will most assuredly be affected.

A special ethical consideration arises when custody mediation reaches an impasse. In most types of mediation, the process is terminated when an impasse is reached and some other form of resolution sought (arbitration or litigation). In custody mediation, particularly in court settings, a custody recommendation may be requested if the parents are unable to negotiate a settlement. Sometimes, a new person is appointed to make an evaluation and to make custody recommendations based on the evaluation. Other times, the mediator is asked to make recommendations based on observations and impressions garnered from the mediation process, as well as on any additional information that may be obtained. Although this latter approach saves time and avoids potential duplication of effort, it contaminates the mediation process by most definitions of mediation. If it is absolutely necessary for the mediator to make custody recommendations in the event of an impasse, the only ethical way to do so is to inform clients at the outset that the mediator may be using information obtained during the mediation process to formulate such recommendations.

Mediator bias is another ethical consideration in mediation, particularly with children. Joint custody is one area where biases might be present. Mediator bias may result from presumptions about "tender years" or a belief that families should have flexibility in scheduling. Some families have never been flexible or adaptable, and it is not helpful to have someone attempt to make them so. The mediator must identify the family's preferred pattern of functioning and help them find ways to restructure that accommodate their preferred style. Mediators should discuss these or other biases that might affect the conduct of mediation with clients in the orientation session.

Finally, self-determination, a basic concept of mediation, can be applied in a biased manner. Mediators may find themselves pushing self-determination beyond a family's ability to make their own decisions. This might be exhibited by holding an inordinate number of sessions, failing to present arbitration and litigation options, or making the parents feel ashamed if they are unable to reach agreements through mediation.

CONCLUSION

Mediation is not a panacea, and including children is not always the best way to proceed in mediation. However, the presence of all family members in at least some sessions seems to make it easier to address everyone's rights and needs as the family restructures itself.

Dissolution of marriage is ultimately a legal process, but the final judgment and decree does not ensure that the process has addressed the rights and needs of minor children. Mediation provides an opportunity for families to negotiate a fair and equitable settlement of the issues, especially the crucial issues of continued parent-parent, parent-child, and child-child relationships. Although the mediation process focuses on needs and the legal process on rights, the list of children's rights shown in Exhibit 8–1 reflects the goals of successful custody mediation.

Exhibit 8–1 Children's Bill of Rights in Divorce Actions

As the parents proceed with the process of dissolving their marital relationship, they recognize and acknowledge the following minimum rights of their children:

1. The right to a continuing relationship with both parents.
2. The right to be treated as an important human being with unique feelings, ideas, and desires.
3. The right to continuing care and guidance from both parents.
4. The right to know and appreciate what is good in each parent without one parent degrading the other.
5. The right to express love, affection, and respect for each parent without having to stifle that love because of fear of disapproval by the other parent.
6. The right to know that the parents' decision to divorce was not the responsibility of the child.
7. The right not to be a source of argument between the parents.
8. The right to honest answers to questions about the changing family relationships.
9. The right to be able to experience regular and consistent contact with both parents and to know the reason for cancellation of time or change of plans.
10. The right to have a relaxed, secure relationship with both parents without being placed in a position to manipulate one parent against the other.

Source: Adapted and reprinted with permission from Dane County Family Court Counseling Service, Madison, WI.

If the mediator is skilled and knowledgeable, is comfortable working with children, carefully assesses the appropriateness of their presence, and clarifies his or her roles and responsibilities with them, mediation should be an ideal format for focusing on children and their needs and rights in the marital dissolution process.

REFERENCES

Ahrons, C. (1980). Joint custody arrangements in the postdivorce family. *Journal of Divorce*, 189–205.

Berg, A. (1983). The attorney as divorce mediator. *Mediation Quarterly*, 21–28.

Bernard, J.M. (1984). Divorced families and the schools: An interface of systems. In J. Hansen (Ed.), *Family therapy with school-related problems*. Rockville, MD: Aspen Systems Corporation.

Bienenfeld, F. (1980). What the children say about divorce. *Conciliation Courts Review*, 49–50.

Clawar, S. (1983). Popular and professional misconceptions about joint custody. *Conciliation Courts Review*, 27–40.

Cleveland, M., & Irvin, K. (1982). Custody counseling: An alternative intervention. *Journal of Marital and Family Therapy*, 105–113.

Committee on the Family Group for the Advancement of Psychiatry (1980). *Divorce, child custody and the family*. New York: Mental Health Materials Center.

Coogler, O.J. (1978). *Structured mediation in divorce settlement*. Lexington, MA: D.C. Heath.

Coulson, R. (1983). *Fighting fair family mediation will work for you*. New York: Free Press.

Haynes, J.M. (1981). *Divorce mediation*. New York: Springer.

Kantor, D., & Vickers, M.I. (1983). Divorce along the family life cycle. In J. Hansen (Ed.), *Clinical implications of the family life cycle*. Rockville, MD: Aspen Systems Corporation.

Kaslow, F. (1981). Divorce and divorce therapy. In A. Gurman & D. Kniskern (Eds.), *Handbook of family therapy*. New York: Brunner/Mazel.

Kelly, J.B. (1983). Mediation and psychotherapy: Distinguishing the differences. *Mediation Quarterly*, 33–44.

Milne, A. (1978). Custody of children in a divorce process: A family self determination model. *Conciliation Courts Review*, 1–10.

Pearson, J., Ring, M.L., & Milne, A. (1983). A portrait of divorce mediation services in the public and private sector. *Conciliation Courts Review*, 1–24.

Rofes, E. (Ed.). (1981). *The kids' book of divorce*. Lexington: Lewis.

Saposnek, D.T. (1983). Strategies in child custody mediation: A family systems approach. *Mediation Quarterly*, 29–54.

Vanderkooi, L., & Pearson, J. (1983). Mediating divorce disputes: Mediator behaviors, styles and roles. *Family Relations*, 557–566.

Wallerstein, J.S., & Kelly, J.B. (1980). *Surviving the breakup*. New York: Basic Books.

Zilbach, J. (1982). Young children in family therapy. In A. Gurman (Ed.), *Questions and answers in family therapy* (Vol. 2). New York: Brunner/Mazel.

9. Legal Considerations for Mental Health Professional Mediators

Catherine G. Crockett

One very real concern of mental health professional mediators who are mediating with couples in the areas of separation, divorce, and postdivorce custody disputes is how to avoid the unlawful activities of practicing law or giving legal advice in their mediation. In most states, mediators are subject to misdemeanor or contempt charges if they are shown to be engaging in the unauthorized practice of law (Silberman, 1982).

Couples working with mental health professional mediators rarely understand when their questions require legal advice. Therefore, the mediator must make that determination. Mediators must understand clearly what is the "practice of law" as it relates to the mediation process and at what point they are giving legal advice or providing legal services. In order to avoid allegations of unauthorized practice of law, mental health professionals have five options. They can

1. recommend that legal advice or independent legal counsel be obtained
2. provide only legal information
3. recommend that the couple see an independent expert for information
4. utilize structured mediation or other model
5. co-mediate with an attorney mediator

LEGAL ADVICE/LEGAL COUNSEL

At the first mediation session, couples usually ask about the role attorneys play in the mediation process: Will attorneys be present at sessions? Will each party need to hire an attorney? There are several schools of thought concerning the attorney's role during the mediation process.

In 1983, the Family Law Section Council of the American Bar Association adopted Standards of Practice for Family Mediators. These standards provide that "the mediator shall inform the participants that each should employ independent legal counsel for advice throughout the mediation process" (p. 456). In interpreting this standard, Bishop (1984), the principal author of the standards, stated that "though falling short of requiring the participants each to have counsel, this is a clear statement that the participants are better served if each has legal advice before decisions are made" (p. 464). This enables the clients to understand not only the law, but also its application to them. Although the American Bar Association intended these standards to apply to mental health professional mediators as well as attorney mediators, the standards are only recommendations. At this time, they do not have the binding force of law.

The Association of Family and Conciliation Courts completed Standards for Practice: Family and Divorce Mediation in May 1984. These standards provide that a mediator should advise parties to seek independent legal advice (1) if it appears that either party's legal rights may be affected, (2) before all the issues are resolved, and (3) when a legal agreement is to be formalized.

Another school of thought on the attorney role in mediation was developed by Coogler (1978) as part of his structured mediation model. He recommended that the mediator and the couple meet with an impartial advisory attorney after the couple has reached tentative agreements on all issues. At that time, the couple may ask any questions that arose during the mediation concerning the divorce process, the law, or tax ramifications of their agreements. After making any necessary adjustments or refinements to the tentative agreements, the advisory attorney drafts the separation and property settlement agreement. If any controversy arises between the parties over advice given by the advisory attorney, the attorney is required to withdraw from the case.

This model has met with mixed responses from the bar associations of different states. The major objection is that impartial advisory attorneys cannot exercise proper loyalty to their clients (i.e., the husband and wife), particularly when the spouses' interests are or may be in opposition or when the case is complex and has varying tax implications. In such situations, opponents of the advisory attorney role claim that attorneys, in violation of their ethical responsibility to provide zealous representation to their clients, are unable to exercise independent legal judgment in the interest of their clients. Despite these objections, several bar associations, including the Oregon State Bar (Proposed Opinion 79-46) (1980) and the Boston Bar (Opinion 78-1) (1978), have concluded that the impartial advisory attorney role is permissible. They have taken the position that the attorney is not "representing" either party and, therefore, does not come within the confines of the American Bar Association disciplinary rule that precludes attorneys from representing clients with more than slightly varying or differing interests. The Oregon and Boston opinions, however, require that impartial advisory attorneys make it clear to their clients that they are not representing either or both of them and further require that they obtain the client's informed consent.

Regardless of the school of thought adopted by a mediator, the benefits of having couples obtain legal advice are considerable. In effect, the attorney acts as a valuable safety net (double when each party has independent counsel) for the mediator and ensures that the parties' decisions are based on inrormed consént.

LEGAL INFORMATION/LEGAL ADVICE

It is my opinion that a mediator may provide a couple with certain types of legal information during the mediation process without risking a charge of the unauthorizèd practice of law. Since the Code of Professional Responsibility of the American Bar Association does not provide a definition of "practice of law," I propose the following definition:

> The practice of law is (1) the giving of legal advice to a client that requires (a) a knowledge of the law and (b) the exercise of legal judgment such that an individual can rely on it for taking a course of action; and/or (2) the drafting of legal documents.

Types of legal information that do not constitute the unauthorized practice of law include information pertaining to the workings of the court system, the statutory grounds for divorce, and any other definition provided by statute.

John B., a mental health professional mediator, is mediating with Tom and Donna Simms. The Simms have a 7-year-old daughter, Samantha, and a 16-year-old son, Lee. During the first mediation session, Donna asks John the legal age of majority in the District of Columbia. John B. responds that 18 is the age of majority in the District of Columbia.

The information given by John B., which is a matter of public record, does not constitute the unauthorized practice of law. If, however, the Simms had asked John whether they could live in the same house and be legally separated for purposes of obtaining a divorce in the District of Columbia and if John had responded that they could, John would have given unauthorized legal advice; his response required the application of District of Columbia case law to the Simms' particular situation. John should respond that they have raised a legal question that must be answered by an attorney.

A mediator can provide clients with information pertaining to Social Security entitlements.

Tom Simms has worked for his company long enough to be able to draw Social Security benefits at retirement. In discussing the pension issue with the Simms, John B. asks how long the Simms have been married and suggests that they find out whether Donna Simms, as an ex-spouse, will be entitled to benefits at Tom Simms' retirement or disability. Without engaging in unauthorized practice, the mediator advises the Simms that, as he understands it, ex-spouses have entitlements to Social Security benefits if the spouses were married longer than 10 years. The mediator

also gives the Simms the free pamphlet published by the Social Security
Administration on the Social Security entitlements of a divorced couple.

Mediators may use resource materials to provide couples with legal
information without engaging in the unauthorized practice of law. For
example, the Internal Revenue Service has published a booklet, Tax Information for Divorced or Separated Individuals, that explains filing status,
dependency exemptions, the criteria for alimony, the deductibility of alimony, child support, and property settlements. This publication is free from
any IRS regional office that carries forms and other publications. In many
states, private interest groups publish booklets on the permissible grounds
for divorce, residency requirements (e.g., how long an individual must
reside in that state before being able to file for a divorce), and the steps that
must be taken to satisfy those grounds for divorce. Such resource materials
allow couples to do their own homework.

The Simms, having worked out their custody arrangements, are concerned about their respective tax filing status, both before and after their
divorce. John B. lends them a copy of the IRS publication and points out
the filing status sections. He also explains that, according to the IRS
booklet, filing jointly generally provides the best tax rate for separated
couples before the divorce and that, although they must file separate
returns after the divorce, their tax rate will be lower if one or both of them
qualifies for head of household filing status.

Obviously, it will be difficult in some instances for the mediator to
determine whether the answer calls for legal advice or factual legal information. It is always advisable for the mediator to err on the side of caution and
recommend legal counsel if in doubt.

UTILIZATION OF EXPERTS

Experts, such as accountants, tax attorneys, actuaries, and financial/
investment planners, can provide invaluable assistance to couples who are
without the information or skills necessary to resolve the issues in mediation. When an expert is needed, the mediator should recommend that the
spouses together employ someone totally independent, without any bias or
possible conflict of interest. Through joint meetings, such an expert helps
the couple build a common information base with which to resolve their
problems. The expert is able to explore all the pros and cons of options

available to the couple, provide them with whatever information they need to make appropriate decisions, or offer an informed professional opinion on the probable consequences of the decisions they are making.

In the mediation process, a couple generally has the greatest need for expert advice in the area of tax considerations. To avoid unnecessary confusion and complexity in tax considerations, it is best for the couple to establish the parameters of fair and reasonable agreements in custody, property division, and child and spousal support. After reaching tentative agreements in these areas, the mediator should refer the couple to a tax expert; then the couple and the mediator should reexamine those agreements in light of the expert's advice. The couple should be apprised early in the mediation process that this approach will be utilized. This will help to prevent the entrenchment of either spouse in any particular agreement if changes are later required.

> The Simms have determined that it is best at this time for the children to remain principally in the family home with Donna but to spend about one-third of their time with Tom at his new home. They have done a complete financial work-up with the mediator and tentatively agreed that Donna needs approximately $900.00 per month ($10,800 per annum) for her support and another $400.00 ($4,800 per annum) for the children's support. Donna's salary as a private secondary school teacher is $14,000.00 and Tom's salary as a company manager is $45,000. At this time, John B., the mediator, explains to the couple that according to his understanding child support cannot be deducted by the payer for tax purposes nor is it considered income to the payee. In contrast, alimony can be deducted by the payer and is income to the payee. He further explains that where there is a significant disparity in the incomes of the two spouses a couple can make more income disposable to their family and reduce their total tax payments by placing taxable income in the tax return of the spouse who has the lowest tax rate. In this case, when filing a separate return, Donna has a significantly lower tax rate than Tom. By paying Donna $10,800 in alimony annually, Tom will be able to deduct the entire amount and make substantial tax savings. John B. adds that, in addition to the $10,800 payment, Tom would also include monies to cover Donna's additional tax burden. He also notes it is his understanding that alimony payments exceeding $10,000 per annum must last for more than six years to be deductible. Therefore, the Simms must seriously consider the issue of the length of the payments. (Before January 1, 1985, the mediator would have recommended that the Simms consider a Lester Plan for support payments, but the Lester Plan has been eliminated by the 1984 Tax Reform Act.)

At this point, John B. asks the Simms whether they are interested in exploring this tax avenue with an expert. If they are, John B. recommends names of several attorneys or CPAs who specialize in divorce issues.

Once the Simms obtain the necessary tax advice, they should return to the mediator to discuss that information and decide whether they wish to incorporate that information by modifying or adding to their tentative agreements.

STRUCTURED MEDIATION/OTHER MODELS

One model of mediation, called structured mediation, provides a supportive framework for mental health professional mediators who wish to avoid any appearance of "engaging in the practice of law." Structured mediation is based on specific rules and guidelines to settle the issues of custody, property division, and support. Coogler (1978), who developed the structured mediation model, examined the Uniform Marriage and Divorce Act and the divorce laws of all states that had made comprehensive changes in their divorce laws between 1973 and 1978. He then produced a set of marital mediation rules that reflect the most advanced and enlightened state laws. These rules constitute a private body of law with which to resolve divorce mediation issues.

The basic premise underlying structured mediation is that an individual's right to contract supersedes state law. The U.S. Constitution, Article 1, Section 10 provides: "No State shall pass any law impairing the obligation of contracts." Thus, couples are free to make any contractual agreements that they wish, as long as their agreements do not violate public policy or federal law. In the area of divorce, this generally means that couples may decide the custody, property division, and support issues as they believe is fair and best for their families.

Couples are not required to apply state divorce laws. Rather, state divorce laws are guidelines that the courts must apply when couples are unable to reach an agreement; these laws can also serve as guidelines or criteria for out-of-court settlements. Generally, when couples reach agreement on all issues and execute a separation and property settlement agreement, the only input from the state is at the hearing for a final divorce. At that time, the courts review custody agreements to determine that they are in the best interest of the minor children. In a few states, the courts may also review the property settlement and may change it if the division was not equitable. In practice, however, the courts rarely, if ever, require changes in the custody or property division arrangements that the parties have contracted.

> The Simms have contracted to work out all mediation issues under the marital mediation rules. In the property division session, they identify all items of sole property and marital property. Under the marital mediation rules, marital property is defined as all property acquired by either or both spouses during the marriage, with the exception of gifts to either party, inheritances, and property excluded by valid agreement of the spouses. John B. asks Tom and Donna whether either of them has a pension. Donna states that she has no pension. Tom states that he has a pension, but that it is his sole property. John B. responds that, under the marital mediation rules, Tom's pension benefits constitute Tom's sole property for the years he worked prior to marriage, but that Donna has an interest in the pension benefits for the years he worked during the marriage.

In my view, utilization of the marital mediation rules or other sets of rules developed in other mediation models prevents mediators from falling into the trap of interpreting state divorce statutes to couples and thereby engaging in the unauthorized practice of law.

CO-MEDIATION

Two co-mediators may be used during the divorce mediation process. One co-mediation model (Gold, 1982) requires that one mediator be a mental health professional and the other be an attorney. Mental health professional mediators utilizing this co-mediation model refer questions that contain legal considerations to their attorney mediator counterpart.

> Mike T., a mental health professional, and Sarah R., an attorney, are co-mediating the division of property issue with John and Sandra Linton. The Lintons have severe financial difficulties; instead of having assets to divide, they have only marital debts. Many of their debts are on joint credit cards. One option is for each to assume responsibility for part of the debt. Sandra asks the mediators if, under that option, she can still be sued by a creditor for any part of the debt that John assumes. Sarah R. answers that, under the laws of that state, the Lintons are individually and jointly liable for their debts and that either could be sued by a creditor if the other failed to make payments. Sarah R. further explains that a legal concept often utilized to remedy these situations is a hold-harmless clause. Such a contractual clause provides that, if either party is sued by

a creditor on debts assumed by the other, that party is legally entitled to repayment of all costs and expenses incurred from the suit. Sarah R. recommends that the Lintons use such a clause in their final separation and property settlement agreement if they are concerned about future liability of that nature.

Sarah R. is indeed offering the Lintons legal advice, but she is an attorney. In this case, the couple benefits from the information provided and may pursue this advice further with their counsel.

CONCLUSIONS

To my knowledge, no state or local bar association has brought suit against a mental health professional mediator for unauthorized practice of law. Moreover, I am aware of only one instance in which a bar association has threatened such action. In 1981, Michael Werle, a psychologist in Warwick, Rhode Island, advertised divorce mediation services. Shortly thereafter, the Unauthorized Practice of Law Committee of the Rhode Island Bar Association wrote to Mr. Werle, requesting that he cease and desist from his mediation activities and stating that, in the event he refused this request, his case would be sent to the Rhode Island State Attorney General for prosecution. Mr. Werle sued the Rhode Island Bar Association in federal district court for inhibiting his First Amendment rights of free speech and association. The court ruled that it did not have jurisdiction because the case did not present a federal issue. Currently, this case is on appeal to the U.S. Court of Appeals for the First Circuit. Despite this inauspicious beginning, however, other mental health professionals in Rhode Island have continued to provide mediation services. In fact, the Rhode Island Family Court sponsored a pilot mediation project from January through June 1984.

Other incidents involving alleged unauthorized practice of law have been reported, although they did not lead to legal actions. They involved situations in which a mediator (1) drafted a contract that had financial implications for the couple's property settlement, (2) drafted the couple's agreements into a separation and property settlement agreement, (3) advised a wife that she was ineligible for alimony, and (4) gave erroneous legal advice concerning the substance and application of a state's statutory provisions regarding alimony. All these situations, in my opinion, constitute unauthorized practice of law. Although these cases were resolved informally, it is clear that mediators must remain within their mediation role and avoid even the slightest appearance of unauthorized practice of law.

REFERENCES

Association of Family and Conciliation Courts (1984). *Model standards for practice: Family and divorce mediation.*

Bishop, T.A. (1984). The standards of practice for family mediation: An individual interpretation and comments. *Family Law Quarterly, 17*(4), 461–468.

Coogler, O.J. (1978). *Structured mediation in divorce settlements.* Lexington, MA: D.C. Heath.

Family Law Section Council of the American Bar Association (1984). Standards of practice for family mediators. *Family Law Quarterly, 17*(4), 455–460.

Gold, L. (1982). The psychological context of the interdisciplinary co-mediation team model in marital dissolution. *Conciliation Courts Review, 20*(2), 45–53.

Silberman, L.J. (1982). Professional responsibility problems of divorce mediation. *Family Law Quarterly, 16*(2).

10. The Education and Training of Mediators

Elizabeth Koopman

Aᴌᴛʜᴏᴜɢʜ ᴛʜᴇ ꜰɪᴇʟᴅ ᴏꜰ ᴅɪᴠᴏʀᴄᴇ ᴍᴇᴅɪᴀᴛɪᴏɴ ɪꜱ ɪɴ ɪᴛꜱ ᴇᴀʀʟʏ ꜱᴛᴀɢᴇꜱ of development, it is evolving at a rapid rate. Because the great majority of both the proponents and the opponents of mediation have their primary professional identities in diverse fields and because the divorce-related decisions inherent in the mediation process are multiple and complex, the field has a robust interdisciplinary aura that generates a much needed skepticism and careful scrutiny. The educational programs that are evolving within this dynamic milieu both reflect and shape the evolution of the field.

THE COMPREHENSIVE FOUNDATIONS OF DIVORCE MEDIATION

Divorce mediation has legal, emotional, financial, social, familial, professional, and personal ramifications (Bohannan, 1970). Mediators, especially those in the private sector, often attempt to resolve multiple divorce-related issues that require knowledge from diverse disciplinary bases. Therefore, it is important to conceptualize the mediation process and the education of mediators within a comprehensive framework of interrelated tasks.

While divorce mediation has legitimately been characterized as a process that focuses on the future well-being of divorcing families, it is important to acknowledge that divorce is both a termination and a commencement. Divorce decisions necessitate both a wisdom of hindsight and a wisdom of foresight. The successful resolutions of the tasks of divorce reflect this delicate balance of looking back and planning ahead. Viable postdivorce roles, responsibilities, and relationships reflect, incorporate, and transcend previous roles and responsibilities.

Individual family characteristics—such as financial resources; ages, health, and skills of spouses; numbers, ages, and needs of children; and the nature of extended family relationships—influence the importance and magnitude of the necessary tasks. Mediators may not be overtly or directly involved in all the six basic divorce tasks (Table 10–1), yet they must be knowledgeable about them and must be skilled in helping spouses successfully complete these tasks. In order to do this, the mediator should be able to consult with other professionals whose expertise strengthens comprehensive, viable, and equitable decisions.

While the basic mediation tasks may at first appear merely to mirror the traditional divorce tasks of "division of property, child and spousal support, and custody and visitation," a closer scrutiny of both the in-depth nature of

Table 10–1 Six Basic Divorce Tasks

Basic Tasks	Common Specific Activities	Customary Time Frame	Possible Parties to the Process
1. Divide and distribute material and monetary assets and liabilities	Itemizing financial, material assets and liabilities Establishing ownership (i.e., determining individual and marital property) Assessing needs and rights of family members Determining postdivorce ownership	Before the divorce decree Postdivorce modifications in cases of children's changing needs	Spouses, attorneys, mediators, financial planners and evaluators, CPAs
2. Terminate spousal financial dependence and create financial independence	Assessing current and future material and educational needs of family members Formulating budgets for equitable and optimal fulfillment of needs Articulating agreements for shared responsibility for child support Articulating agreements for support of dependent spouse toward goal of financial independence	Before the divorce Limited postdivorce interventions and activities of approximately 1–4 years	Spouses, attorneys, mediators, financial experts, educational and career counselors

3. Terminate spousal emotional dependence and create emotional independence	Assessing activities and behaviors that reflect continuing spousal emotional dependence Making plans to terminate attachment behaviors Making plans for separate spousal social activities	Predivorce assessment and decisions Long-term commitment, possible reevaluations	Spouses, mediators, counselors, therapists, clergy, support groups
4. Restructure and reallocate parental roles and relationships	Changing co-parental relationship from affectional to businesslike Articulating and fulfilling modified postdivorce parental roles and responsibilities, focusing on physical needs of the children as well as parental needs Incorporating assessment of needs, wants, capacities, constraints of all family members a) Specifying children's residential, educational, medical, religious, recreational plans	Preseparation and ongoing, especially during years of children's dependency	Parents, mediators, counselors, parent education professionals, school personnel, appropriately aged children, appropriate members of extended families

Table 10–1 continued

Basic Tasks	Common Specific Activities	Customary Time Frame	Possible Parties to the Process
	b) Specifying particular parental roles for shared nurturance, residential and financial responsibilities		
	c) Establishing rules or guidelines for parent contacts		
	d) Establishing rules or guidelines for parent-child contacts		
	e) Making agreements for emergencies		
5. Build and support the relationships with each parent, siblings, extended family	Overtly acknowledging the rights and needs of children to loving relationships and activities with all family members	Preseparation and continuing indefinitely	Parents, children when appropriate, mediators, counselors, stepparents, grandparents, clergy, support groups
	Establishing guidelines for decision making re time with special family members, special family occasions		
	Eliminating negative evaluation of family members before children and other family members		

| 6. Plan and prepare for future life changes that entail modifications of roles/agreements | Articulating predictable developmental changes in children's needs and capacities

Articulating possible changes in spouses' lives (e.g., marital status, employment, residence)

Defining procedures and principles to follow when modification needs arise (e.g., mediation of future changes and conflicts) | At divorce decree and continuing, especially while children are dependent | Spouses, mediators, attorneys, counselors, children when appropriate |

the objectives and the activities customarily required to accomplish the objectives reveals a decision-making process that goes far beyond mere negotiating and bargaining activities. It engages the parties and the mediator in extensive discussions and deliberation regarding the needs and well-being of an evolving family constellation. The agreement document itself, detailing such items as distribution of funds, payments of bills, holiday plans, school placements, and residential arrangements, evolves from a careful creative process far different from a series of compromises (Fisher & Ury, 1983) and far different from the customary therapeutic or legal interventions utilized with divorcing families (Kelly, 1983; Koopman & Hunt, 1983; Milne, 1983). Consequently, professional mediation education is unique in its combination of multiple interdisciplinary components. Moreover, the accomplished mediator is so well acquainted with these components as to be able to weave them skillfully into the formulation and testing of the agreement.

DEVELOPMENT OF DIVORCE MEDIATION CURRICULA

Excellence in education and training in the field of divorce mediation is predicated on (1) the determination of essential knowledge bases, (2) the delineations of specific applied skills, (3) the establishment of pedagogical programs that lead to competency in the critical areas, and (4) the implementation of research studies that examine the effectiveness of ongoing activities and generate new knowledge and theory in the field.

Decisions relating to 1) the determination of critical *content areas* and 2) the subsequent determination of the *extent of coverage* of those subject matters are basic to curriculum development. There is some, albeit limited, disagreement in the divorce mediation field regarding which are the essential content areas. It is the observation of this author that the disputants in the issue of content areas are predominantly those persons who closely and narrowly identify divorce mediation with their primary profession, "individuals who . . . due to the seeming, though misleading, resemblance of the divorce mediator's role to their own professional role, make the casual assumption that they already possess the knowledge and skills to serve as a divorce mediator" (Koopman & Hunt, 1983, p. 31). Such persons take the position that "solely a legal education/solely a clinical counseling education/or solely a negotiation/arbitration background" is needed for divorce mediation competencies. There is increasing evidence, however, gleaned from discussions at professional meetings, from reading the professional periodic literature, and currently from initial data analyses of a divorce mediation curriculum survey of professors in a variety of relevant graduate academic units in higher education (Koopman, Boskey, & Gorman, 1984) of considerable agreement regarding the importance of a broad interdisciplinary knowledge base which incorporates subject matter regarding law, finance, family, adult and child development, and conflict theory in addition to knowledge and skill in techniques of communication, negotiation, and mediation. (Koopman, 1984, pp. 3–4)

An essential part of curriculum development, in addition to the delineation of content areas, is the determination of appropriate learning activities and their appropriate sequence within the total learning experience. A proposed sequence for divorce mediators is (1) the acquisition of the basic substantive knowledge, (2) skill development via simulations, (3) supervised practicum experiences, and (4) continuing professional development (Association of Family and Conciliation Courts, 1983). Table 10–2 illustrates this overall conceptualization.

CURRENT STATUS OF EDUCATION AND TRAINING PROGRAMS

Because divorce mediation is still in its infancy, because there is no established and comprehensive professional mediation network, and because private practices, court services, training experiences, and academic programs are rapidly proliferating, it is impossible to construct a complete profile of the current status of education and training in divorce mediation. However, an interdisciplinary research project under the cooperative sponsorship of the American Association of Law Schools and the Association of Family and Conciliation Courts is presently being conducted to document the development of educational programs in the divorce mediation field (Koopman, Boskey, & Gorman, 1984). University professors and private trainers are being asked to rate in importance the following educational components:

1. child development
2. adolescent development

Table 10–2 Professional Divorce Mediation Education: Key
Components, Educative Modes, and Sequencing

	Substantive Knowledge Base	Skill Training

C
 	
O
 	
N
 	
T
 	
E
 	
N
 	
T
	Human development
	  1. Child and adult development
	  2. Family systems theory
	  3. The divorce experience
	Theories of conflict and conflict
	  resolution
	Family law
	  1. Judicial procedures
	  2. Divorce law—jurisdictional
	     issues and variations
	Family finances
	  1. Property division (e.g., real
	     estate, pensions, invest-
	     ments, professional prac-
	     tices, and education)
	  2. Spousal and child support
	     issues (e.g., maintenance
	     and rehabilitation)
	  3. Future financial respon-
	     sibility (e.g., wills, trusts,
	     insurance, investments)
	Referral resources in the
	  community; interprofessional
	  linkages
	Professional ethics
	Communication and negotiation
	  skills
		"In-house" skill development via
		  role plays, canned case
		  analysis, observation of
		  mediation including
		  supervision, feedback for
		  refinement of skills

M
 	
O
 	
D
 	
E
	College and university
	  coursework
	Professional development
	  workshops and seminars
	Professional independent study
	  with tutoring
	Professional meetings in law,
	  finance, social work, mediation,
	  counseling, education, therapy
		College and university course-
		  work
		Comprehensive skills
		  development workshops with
		  practicing professionals

Skill Practice	Continuing Education, Professional Development, and Professional Contribution
Intern/practicum experiences: actual service delivery with clients under closely supervised conditions	
College and university internships in public or private sectors	Additional coursework
Co-mediation with experienced mediator in public or private sectors	Professional meetings, workshops, seminars
	Peer supervision
	Active participation in professional groups
	Pro bono work in interdisciplinary teams
	Speaking engagements to professional and community groups
	Legislative work/public policy

3. adult development
4. family dynamics
5. the psychological aspects of divorce
6. theories of conflict resolution
7. divorce law
8. family budgeting
9. property division
10. tax consequences
11. professional referral sources
12. communication and negotiation skills
13. professional ethics
14. supervised internships

While the researchers are still actively involved in the refinement of the survey instrument and an initial data collection is still in progress, the data obtained thus far provide some preliminary insights into the present attitudes of academicians ($N = 16$, 9 law professors, 7 professors in the behavioral and social science fields) and private trainers ($N = 8$; 2 trainers with JDs, 3 with PhDs, 3 with MAs in social science). As a group, 75% of the surveyed academicians rated 12 of the 14 items as either "Very Important" or "Essential," and 75% of the private trainers viewed 7 of the 14 items as "Very Important" or "Essential." Items that 75% of all persons surveyed rated as "Very Important" or "Essential" were divorce law, psychological aspects of divorce, communication and negotiating skills, professional ethics, and supervised internship. Three areas distinguished the academicians from the private trainers: (1) developmental knowledge (child, adolescent, adult), (2) family dynamics, and (3) outside professional resources for referral. Although 75% of the academicians rated these as "Very Important" or "Essential," the private trainers placed less emphasis on them. This difference may be a function of the massive time constraints on private training programs or may be an indication that academicians tend to think more in terms of comprehensive professional education as they evaluate educational quality.

While it is premature to predict the course of development of academic programs in the field of divorce mediation,

three curricular patterns seem evident at the moment: 1) limited coverage of mediation related topics in existing/traditional courses, 2) creation of a single one semester "Divorce Mediation" course in which most topics are incorporated, and 3) creation of "programs or concentrations" in which the topics are covered in four or more "core courses," plus relevant "supporting" courses.

The first pattern, i.e., subtopic coverage in traditional courses seems common in law schools. Present observations indicate, for instance, that in law schools the "mediation relevant contents" cited above tend to have at least cursory mention in one or two courses, i.e., "family law" or "dispute resolution." Thus limited or peripheral coverage of the content areas outside the strictly legal aspects of marital dissolution seems currently to be the modal practice. In behavioral and social science departments also the content areas are currently covered as limited topics within more general courses such as Marriage and Divorce Therapy, Family Decision Making, Relational Communications, etc.

The second curriculum pattern, i.e., coverage of most relevant topics in a newly constructed single course on "Divorce Mediation" seems to be emerging when two different academic units, e.g., Law and Social Work, collaborate via co-teaching and interdisciplinary student enrollment in the "divorce mediation course." Such a course may be an "elective" for students in law, psychology, social work, etc. (LaFortune, 1983; Stier & Hamilton, 1984; Trombletta, 1983).

The third curriculum pattern, i.e., a *program* or *concentration* in family/divorce mediation, is currently evolving within behavioral and social science disciplines. Such "multiple course models" may represent a "concentration" within a graduate degree program or a post graduate specialty area for practicing professionals (The Department of Human Development, the University of Maryland, 1983; The Department of Human Development and Family Ecology, the University of Illinois, 1983; the Center for Family Studies, the Catholic University of America, 1983). Students take several separate but complementary courses such as "Theories of Conflict Resolution," "Family Law," "Family Systems Theory," "Family Finance," "Techniques of Conflict Resolution in Divorce Mediation," and "Internship in Divorce Mediation." At the moment the future of these three curricular patterns is unclear, but each merits scrutiny and evaluation by academicians as the divorce mediation field evolves. (Koopman, 1984)

There is much variation in private training programs as well. The time periods of training seem to vary from 1 to 7 days, with 2-day or 5-day programs being the most common. All the private trainers who have so far responded to the curriculum survey report that their programs cover (1) communication and negotiating skills, (2) divorce law, and (3) family budgeting (Koopman, Boskey, & Gorman, 1984). The time allotted to each in the various training programs varies considerably, however; for example, the communication and negotiating skills component varies from 1½ to 20 hours. The coverage of the other topics varies from 15 minutes to 3 hours. All respondents reported some time spent in skill development simulations or role plays; about one-half are trying to offer some sort of supervision after the initial training programs. Supervisory modes include discussing cases with experienced mediators and sending audiotapes of mediation sessions to be critiqued by a geographically distant supervisor. While 75% of the trainers rated supervision as "Very Important" or "Essential," the unavailability of practicum sites and the geographical distance between trainee and supervisor remain problems.

There has been and will continue to be considerable discussion of the future roles of both academic and private training programs (Folberg & Taylor, 1984; Koopman, 1984; Koopman & Hunt, 1983; Milne, 1983; Sander, 1983). Respondents in the current curriculum survey were asked for their thoughts on these future roles. All the academicians expressed the opinion that higher education will and ought to become increasingly important; they anticipate an expansion in university teaching and research in the field. Of the private training respondents, one-third feel that universities should have limited or no involvement. The general opinion among the other private training respondents and among the academicians is that private training programs will evolve into postgraduate professional development workshops in which trained and experienced mediators refine skills, update knowledge, and share professional expertise. The research data thus corroborate the recommendations of Folberg and Taylor (1984):

> Although these workshops provide a valuable training opportunity, they should not be oversold. The time restrictions imposed on a training format of one week or less limit their role to mediation orientation, an introduction to substantive knowledge, and skill refinement. They should not be regarded as comprehensive curricula. . . . It is anticipated that more law schools and other graduate and undergraduate departments will offer courses in mediation concepts and skills. (pp. 235–236)

An enlarged university role in the field of divorce mediation seems inevitable. While the structures and expectations within institutions of higher education predispose them toward (1) quality control, (2) established traditions of ethics and equity, (3) program stability, (4) controlled costs, (5) availability of educational materials, and (6) comprehensive integration of research with teaching and service delivery, such higher education problems as narrow administrative structures, territorial combativeness among disciplines, and an excessive emphasis on publication over teaching and service obstruct academic program development (Koopman, 1984).

CRITICAL CONTEMPORARY ISSUES

The creation of excellence in professional practice in any field depends on the creation of excellence in professional education and training. Beyond defining curricular content and identifying appropriate educational experiences, some special challenges must be addressed in the education of mediators:

1. problems inherent in the education of heterogeneous adult learners
2. the development of cooperative professional relationships in an interdisciplinary field
3. the creation of research studies to evaluate the efficacies of educational programs and to generate new knowledge

Since divorce mediators currently enter the field as professionals with background, experience, and training in another professional discipline, educators and trainers must be prepared to work with a group of learners who bring unique combinations of both assets and liabilities to their learning experiences.

A pressing pedagogical issue in the education of divorce mediators, and one to which insufficient attention has been paid thus far, concerns the creation of appropriate contents and viable pedagogical practices for a heterogeneous group of adult learners who are likely to have discrepant preestablished professional values and mind sets, deeply ingrained and both appropriate and inappropriate professional techniques, and significant gaps in some of the critical areas of knowledge. . . . For students of mediation who come to their mediation study and training from a strong background in specialized fields such as law, counseling, therapy, psychology, etc. there exists a need for a tremendous amount of both learning and unlearning to take place. In Piagetian terms, a great deal of assimilation of new knowledge needs to take place but also a great deal of accommodation, i.e., the modification of pre-existing cognitive and attitudinal formulations which are not appropriate to the mediation of familial conflicts. (Koopman, 1984)

Interprofessional differences and problems of philosophy and practice of mediators who enter the field from a previous professional discipline are receiving more and more attention (Callner, 1977; Folberg & Taylor, 1984; Haynes, 1978, 1981, 1984; Kelly, 1983; Koopman, 1980, 1984; Koopman & Hunt, 1981, 1983; Milne, 1983; Moore, 1983; Silberman, 1981; Wheeler, 1980), but a comprehensive and balanced synthesis of legal and therapeutic education, philosophy, and procedures has not yet been accomplished. Such a synthesis must be based on an assessment of the assets and limitations of the substantive knowledge base, the values, and the philosophies of each discipline, as well as a delineation of common disciplinary procedural issues that affect the mediation process (Tables 10–3 and 10–4). Educators and trainers then need to incorporate these factors in their curriculum development. Four additional issues remain problematic in the evolving interdisciplinary professional conceptualization of the divorce mediation field:

1. professional isolation, e.g., lack of knowledge about others' training and expertise and suspicions of the efficacy of the others' practice
2. maintenance of a professional "mystique"
3. inadequate conceptualization of legal, economic, emotional, familial, social, and religious factors of the divorce experience
4. inadequate background in conflict resolution theory and in mediation-specific conflict resolution skills

These issues must be considered in the development of educational curricula.

While interdisciplinary educational experiences provide an unequaled opportunity for comprehensive, in-depth discussions of mediation-relevant topics and set the stage for increased interdisciplinary appreciation and cooperation, it is necessary for students to have some similarities in background before they can be blended into an integrated educational

Table 10–3 Common Assets and Limitations of Legal Education, Philosophy, and Procedures[a]

	Common Assets	*Common Limitations*
Legal education	Knowledge of judicial roles and procedures Knowledge of legal roles and procedures Knowledge of financial issues, e.g., taxes, real estate, insurance, pensions	Limited knowledge of human development factors, e.g., child and adult development, motivation, defense mechanisms, family systems, attachment, the divorce experience Limited knowledge of conflict theory and mediation-specific skills
Philosophical orientation and tendencies	Canon of ethics Concern for legal implications and problems Client advocacy and support	Some legal canons inappropriate for mediation Emphasis on precedent or preestablished standards rather than individualization Translating personal factors into legal issues Single client focus/non-systems orientation Authoritarian control/client dependency Reliance on fault-based thinking Dedication to adversarial model of justice
Procedural factors	Focus on task accomplishment Distancing of self from involvement in client's personal problems Direct professional activity and engagement in the process	Overemphasis on "agreement" Lack of empathic behaviors Failure to attend to or identify significant personal/emotional facts Diminution of client activity and responsibility/over-control/negotiating *for* the client rather than facilitating clients' negotiating

[a]Based on Bethel, 1983.

Table 10–3 continued

Common Assets	Common Limitations
Emphasis on analytic thought	Analysis of behavioral and material factors, to the exclusion of affective influences Making determination on past events/overlooking importance of testing determinations on their viability for the future functioning of restructured family
Routine attention to full disclosure	
Skills in writing, articulating agreements	Reliance on adversarial methods

experience. First, some mechanism should be developed to narrow the discipline-specific gaps in substantive knowledge. Once their backgrounds are sufficiently comparable, shared learning experiences in such areas as conflict theory, communication skills, ethics, and mediation skills (including experiential learning in role plays and simulations) are likely to be challenging and productive.

Two models for implementing this type of educational sequencing are suggested in Table 10–5. Alternative I can be adapted to both the university and private setting; Alternative II is likely to evolve as mediation expands into graduate and professional education programs in the university setting. The viability of both alternatives, indeed the future of the divorce mediation field itself, depends on the development of interdisciplinary and interprofessional cooperation.

It seems likely that educating fellow professionals will prove to be even more of a challenge than educating the public. . . . The interprofessional conflicts over who can mediate and what body will ultimately set the standards will continue to challenge

Table 10–4 Common Assets and Limitations of Therapeutic Education, Philosophy and Procedures[a]

	Common Assets	*Common Limitations*
Therapeutic education	Extensive knowledge of human development factors, e.g., child development, motivation, defense mechanisms, family systems, attachment, the divorce experience, knowledge of models of therapeutic intervention	Limited knowledge of legal and judicial roles and procedures of the specifics and parameters of the law and of financial issues, e.g., taxes, real estate, insurance, pensions Limited knowledge of conflict theory and mediation-specific skills
Philosophical orientations and tendencies	Respect for individualized decisions, individual differences Professional ethics and standards Human service philosophy Developmental/life process perspective	Therapeutic goals Inadequacy of ethics and standards to mediation "Medical model" type orientation
Procedural factors	Attention to emotional dynamics of problem Patience with process of change/decision making Attentiveness to resistance issues Empathic predisposition Skills in interviewing	Overemphasis on internal personal factors Emphasis on process over task (varies with therapeutic model) Lack of directiveness and control of a process Overdiscussion of affective variables Initial focus on strengthening interpersonal "connectedness" not "separateness"

[a]Based on Gray, 1983.

Table 10–4 continued

Common Assets	Common Limitations
Intuitive insight	Encouraging a decision that "feels right"; overlooking pragmatic or legal reality testing and long-term practical implications/ inexperience in working with decisions of legal and permanent finality Inexperienced in time-limited and task-specific interventions (varies with therapeutic model)

us. . . . Practically, professional conflicts between [sic] the disciplines that support mediation may prove quite harmful. A more reasonable approach seems to be that of providing an opportunity for the various disciplines to explore collectively what accounts for good practice. (Milne, 1983, p. 29)

We must avoid fruitless interdisciplinary squabbles about who should do this work . . . that is a bogus question. The work should be done by individuals who possess certain requisite competencies, . . . and we should strive to articulate the minimal competencies and provide individuals with the training that is needed to attain them. (Sander, 1983, p. 7)

In an analogous summary of the current status of divorce mediation, the authors see it currently as the stepchild of family therapy, the adoptee of family law, and the potentially victimized child in a disrupted custody case! Only when divorce mediation is viewed as the legitimate offspring of both professions whose current parental function is to raise and nourish it toward a mature independence, can its healthy growth and development be assured. (Koopman & Hunt, 1983, p. 29)

From a professional development point of view, mediation educators and trainers owe a debt of gratitude to the precedent set by many private trainers and fledgling mediation groups. Private trainers have used interprofessional teams of instructors, and mediation associations have organized themselves

Table 10–5 Possible Models for Interprofessional Education for Divorce Mediators

	1.	2.	3.	4.	5.
I. Postgraduate model for practicing professionals from disparate disciplines	Separate educational experiences in selected substantive knowledge bases: (1) human development factors, (2) family systems, (3) finance, (4) law	Joint educational experiences in conflict theory, referral sources, communication skills, professional ethics	Joint educational experiences in skill development in divorce mediation	Shared or separate practica experiences	Shared professional development experiences
II. Concurrent graduate education model	Substantive knowledge bases covered by students enrolling in appropriate graduate classes that may be outside their own department or college				

around an interdisciplinary membership. Whether disciplinary professional associations and institutions of higher education can follow this worthy precedent remains to be seen.

If given administrative and faculty support, institutions of higher education could establish a complementary and cooperative focus for the legitimate interests and expertise of multiple disciplines (Figure 10–1). The open availability of course offerings in all disciplines would provide a means to acquire many of the core knowledge bases. The various academic units would need to determine if the conflict resolution and divorce mediation

Figure 10–1 An Interdisciplinary Model of Family Dispute Resolution in Higher Education

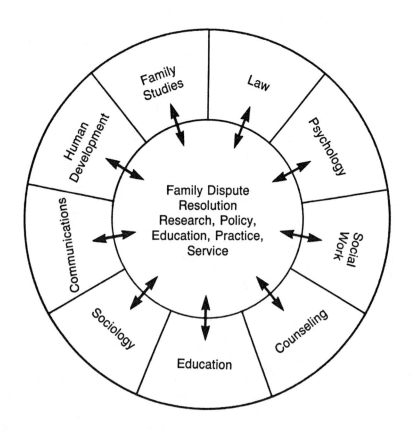

courses could best be housed in one or two units or if they would best be cross-listed and, possibly, team taught. Academicians are vulnerable to the dangers of competitiveness, however; in this era of declining resources, interdisciplinary cooperation may be elusive (The Carnegie Foundation for the Advancement of Teaching, 1982). It would be sad and ironic if those advocating the cooperative conflict resolution mode would undermine that which they seek to support by adopting the antithetical behaviors of competition and territoriality.

Although research in the effectiveness of mediator skills and mediation processes is being developed, the research component of mediation education and training has been almost entirely overlooked. The importance of specific contents, the efficacy of particular pedagogical techniques, and the degree to which these and other variables are translated into quality service delivery remain unclear. It is apparent that progress is being made in articulating curricular contents and in experimenting with education strategies, yet these are only the first steps. Curricular consensus is not necessarily curricular adequacy, and much of the current thinking is still based on unexamined assumptions, untested theories and practices, and, perhaps, unfounded fears. It is now time for educators and trainers to scrutinize and evaluate the results of their efforts. Quality assurance depends on such research evaluations.

REFERENCES

Association of Family and Conciliation Courts. (1983, December). Task group report to the mediation committee at the annual meeting of the Association of Family and Conciliation Courts, Toronto, Canada.

Bethel, C. (1983, October). *Assets and limitations of professional legal education in the development of divorce mediator competencies.* Presentation at the annual meeting of the American Association of Marriage and Family Therapy, Washington, DC.

Bohannan, P. (Ed.). (1970). *Divorce and after: An analysis of the emotional and social problems of divorce.* Garden City, NY: Doubleday.

Callner, B. (1977). Boundaries of the divorce lawyer's role. *Family Law Quarterly, 10,* 389–988.

The Carnegie Foundation for the Advancement of Teaching. (1982). *The control of the campus.* Washington, DC: Author.

The Catholic University of America. (1983). *The post-graduate certificate program in family mediation.* (Available from the National Center for Family Studies, the Catholic University of America, St. John's Hall, Suite 200, Washington, DC 20061.)

The Department of Human Development and Family Ecology. (1983). *Graduate study in family mediation.* (Available from Department of Human Development and Family Ecology, the University of Illinois, Urbana, IL 61801.)

The Department of Human Development, the University of Maryland. (1983). *Current graduate offerings in dispute resolution and divorce mediation.* (Available from Department of Human Development, the University of Maryland, College Park, MD 20742.)

Fisher, R., & Ury, W. (1983). *Getting to yes.* New York: Penguin Books.

Folberg, J., & Taylor, A. (1984). *Mediation: A comprehensive guide to resolving conflicts without litigation.* San Francisco: Jossey-Bass.

Gray, K. (1983, October). *Assets and limitations of professional mental health education in the development of divorce mediator competencies.* Presentation at the annual meeting of the American Association of Marriage and Family Therapy, Washington, DC.

Haynes, J.M. (1978). Divorce mediator: A new role. *Social Work, 23*, January, 5–9.

Haynes, J.M. (1981). *Divorce mediation: A practical guide for therapists and counselors.* New York: Springer.

Haynes, J.M. (1984). A conceptual model of the process of family mediation: Implications for training. In D.H. Olson & B.C. Miller (Eds.), *Family studies review yearbook* (pp. 491–497). Beverly Hills, CA: Sage Publications.

Kelly, J. (1983). Mediation and psychotherapy: Distinguishing the differences. *Mediation Quarterly, 1*, 33–44.

Koopman, E.J. (1980). A survey of academic background, perceived competency, and professional interests in issues of family law of selected senior law school students. Unpublished manuscript.

Koopman, E.J. (1984). The present and future role of higher education in divorce mediation: Problems and promise in teaching, research, and service. *The Journal of Divorce.*

Koopman, E.J., Boskey, J., & Gorman, K. (1984). Divorce mediation curriculum survey: Preliminary analyses. Unpublished manuscript.

Koopman, E.J., & Hunt, E.J. (1981). An evaluation of a five day training program in family mediation. Unpublished manuscript.

Koopman, E.J., & Hunt, E.J. (1983). Divorce mediation: Issues in defining, educating, and implementing a new and needed profession. *Conciliation Courts Review, 21*, 25–37.

LaFortune, F. (1983). Curriculum content in divorce mediation. McGill University. Unpublished manuscript.

Milne, A.L. (1983). Divorce mediation: The state of the art. *Mediation Quarterly, 1*, 15–31.

Moore, C.W. (1983). Training mediations for family dispute resolution. *Mediation Quarterly, 2*, 79–89.

Sander, F.A. (1983). Family mediation: Problems and prospects. *Mediation Quarterly, 2*, 3–31.

Silberman, L. (1981). Professional responsibility: Problems of divorce mediation. *Family Law Reporter, 7*, 4001–4011.

Stier, S., & Hamilton, N. (1984). Family systems and the legal system: A new fit through teaching divorce mediation. University of Iowa, Iowa City. Unpublished manuscript.

Trombletta, D. (1983). Curriculum content in divorce mediation. University of California, Santa Cruz. Unpublished manuscript.

Wheeler, M. (1980). *Divided children.* New York: Summit.

Index to Collections 9-12

HOW TO USE THIS INDEX

The first number following the entry is the Collection number: **9, 10, 11, 12**. The number that follows is the page number within that collection where the reference will be found. For example, **9**/16-17 refers to Collection **9**, pages 16 to 17.

NATIONAL UNIVERSITY LIBRARY

HQ
834
D54
1985
c.2

053176

Divorce and family
mediation

North County Library

DATE DUE

OCT 19 1997		
OCT 20 1999		
JUL 2 2 1999		